THE COMPOSITION OF THE DEUTERONOMISTIC HISTORY

HARVARD SEMITIC MUSEUM

HARVARD SEMITIC MONOGRAPHS

edited by
Frank Moore Cross

Number 35
THE COMPOSITION
OF THE DEUTERONOMISTIC HISTORY
by
Brian Peckham

Brian Peckham

THE COMPOSITION OF THE DEUTERONOMISTIC HISTORY

Scholars Press
Atlanta, Georgia

UNIVERSITY
OF NEW BRUNSWICK

AUG 17 1988

LIBRARIES

THE COMPOSITION OF THE DEUTERONOMISTIC HISTORY

Brian Peckham

© 1985
The President and Fellows of Harvard College

Library of Congress Cataloging in Publication Data

Peckham, Brian.
The composition of the deuteronomistic history.

(Harvard Semitic monographs ; no. 35)
Bibliography: p.
Includes index.
1. D document (Biblical criticism) 2. J Document (Biblical criticism) 3. P document (Biblical criticism) 4. E document (Biblical criticism) 5. Bible. O.T. Pentateuch—Criticism, interpretation, etc. I. Title. II. Series.
BS1181.17.P43 1985 222'.1066 85-11742
ISBN 0-89130-909-8

Printed in the United States of America
on acid-free paper

Publication of this work was made possible
by a grant from Regis College in Toronto

CONTENTS

Preface

This study in the history of Israel's literature resumes diverse intellectual and academic traditions. It reflects on the writing of history and the composition of texts with the attention and interest of an educated reader. It gives consideration to grammar, observes logic and rhetoric, examines the accumulation and connection of meaning, and follows the unfolding of interpretation. The theory it develops tries to leave the text intact for the next reader and the history open to different interpretation.

I am indebted as always to Frank Moore Cross, this time in particular for the publication of my work in the Harvard Semitic Monographs series.

Brian Peckham
Regis College
January, 1985

ABBREVIATIONS

AB	Anchor Bible
AnBib	Analecta Biblica
AOAT	Alter Orient und Altes Testament
ATANT	Abhandlungen zur Theologie des Alten und Neuen Testaments
BASOR	*Bulletin of the American Schools of Oriental Research*
Bib	*Biblica*
BKAT	Biblischer Kommentar: Altes Testament
BTB	*Biblical Theology Bulletin*
BZ	*Biblische Zeitschrift*
BZAW	Beihefte zur Zeitschrift für die alttestamentliche Wissenschaft
CBQ	*Catholic Biblical Quarterly*
ErIsr	*Eretz Israel*
FRLANT	Forschungen zur Religion und Literatur des Alten und Neuen Testaments
HAT	Handbuch zum Alten Testament
HSM	Harvard Semitic Monographs
HTR	*Harvard Theological Review*
JAOS	*Journal of the American Oriental Society*
JBL	*Journal of Biblical Literature*
JJS	*Journal of Jewish Studies*
JSOTSS	Journal for the Study of the Old Testament - Supplement Series
RB	*Revue Biblique*
SBLMS	Society of Biblical Literature Monograph Series
TLZ	*Theologische Literaturzeitung*
TTZ	*Trierer theologische Zeitschrift*
ÜP	Martin Noth, *Überlieferungsgeschichte des Pentateuch*, Stuttgart: W. Kohlhammer, 1948
ÜS	Martin Noth, *Überlieferungsgeschichtliche Studien*, I, Tübingen: Max Niemeyer, 1943
VT	*Vetus Testamentum*

VTS	Vetus Testamentum, Supplements
WMANT	Wissenschaftliche Monographien zum Alten und Neuen Testament
ZAW	*Zeitschrift für die alttestamentliche Wissenschaft*
ZTK	*Zeitschrift für Theologie und Kirche*

INTRODUCTION

Martin Noth thought that the Dtr history was the work of an author and historian.[1] It was composed from written sources by one person with a distinctive style, perspective and theology.[2] It was never revised but subsequently it was attached to the Pentateuch, divided into books, and enhanced with supplements and appendices.[3]

The theory was brilliant but difficult to sustain. Noth himself failed to give it an adequate literary or historical foundation and ultimately reneged on its basic postulates.[4] He compromised his thesis of Dtr authorship by isolating linguistic and literary criteria that were sporadic, adventitious, and typical of an editor.[5] He impugned his theory of a Dtr history by confining historicity to the aetiologies, sources and traditions that it recorded and quoted verbatim.[6] These mistakes and inconsistencies did not diminish the fascination of his theory,[7] but they complicated it and precluded its verification.

The theory can be verified by analyzing the composition of the history and its reference to sources.[8] Its sources were complete literary works that comprised both the components of the Pentateuch (JPE) and an earlier version of the history (Dtr^1). These works were included not simply by citation but with annotation, commentary, criticism and interpretation. They were combined with each other by a system of cross-reference and harmonization and were distributed in the new version of the Pentateuch and the history composed and written by Dtr.^{2} This was a monumental work but it had substantial literary resources and profound historical antecedents.

The first of Dtr^2's literary and historical sources is J. It is fundamental to all the other writings but presumes none of them. The second is the Dtr^1 history: it knows, quotes, and expounds J but is independent of the other sources. The third author is P who rewrote J to balance and correct the Dtr^1 history and interpretation of J. The fourth source is E that contains variants and supplements to J, Dtr^1 and P. The principal author and historian is Dtr^2 who rewrote these sources as the history of Israel from creation to the fall of Jerusalem. This history was not revised but its codification of the law was amended by a legislative supplement (Ps) that gave the Pentateuch its final form.

Chapter 1

THE J NARRATIVE

Noth used the same principles and methods in analyzing the Pentateuch that he had applied to the study of the Dtr history.[9] He thought that all the essential elements of the Pentateuch had coalesced in a pre-literary cultic or confessional phase and that their derivation was determinative of their subsequent development.[10] The Pentateuchal sources, consequently, were mainly selective expressions of a definitive and established tradition which their authors transmitted but did not compose.[11] The sources were neither continuous nor complete but were combined with each other by a succession of redactors who excerpted and arranged them.[12]

Noth's basic mistake consisted in supposing that the sources were fragmentary and discontinuous. Then instead of trying to verify his theory he simply combined it with two others that made it seem plausible. His appeal to a living tradition scrupulously transmitted gave historical substance to the fragmentary texts. The idea of repeated and responsible editing supplied a literary allure to the haphazard and discontinuous history. This analysis ultimately made the sources more abstruse than the literary and historical problems they were meant to resolve. Eventually it became simpler to ignore the theory of sources and concentrate instead either on the tradition[13] or the redaction[14] that made it seem right.

The J source is a complete and continuous narrative history of Israel.[15] It is composed of six episodes and arranged in paragraphs (Fig 1). Each episode tells the story of some hero in the distant past and is distinguished from the others by its introduction and by the patterns of recurrence that define its boundaries. The paragraphs mark the progress of the narrative and are distinguished by their cadence or assonance or some other form of iteration.[16]

The first episode is the story of a man and a woman. It is introduced by seven circumstantial clauses that describe the creation of heaven and earth from the perspective of the farmer and herdsman (Gen 2:4b-6). The first paragraph relates that the land was not tillable and that man lived in a garden planted by God (Gen 2:7a, 8-9, 16-17). The second explains that since the animals were not suitable companions God brought man a woman to be his wife (Gen 2:18-19a[a], 20b-22, 25). The story ends in the third paragraph (Gen 3:1-7a, 8-13, 22-23) when both its major themes have been recapitulated: at first there was no man to till the land (2:5b) but at last man returns to the land to tend it (3:23); in the beginning man is threatened with death (2:17) but in the end he risks living for ever (3:22).

The second episode is connected with the first in the things it supposes and modifies. In the first episodes man and woman ate the food of the Gods and became like God: in the second episode the sons of God found women attractive and married them (Gen 6:1-2, 4a[b]b). The first episode tells the story of man and woman and Yahweh who is called God: the second episode, after the marriages between women and the sons of God, tells the story of another man and Yahweh but omits the name God.[17] In the first episode there was no rain (2:5) but in the second the rain floods the whole world (7:4). The first is the story of man and woman, and the second is the story of Noah, his wife and his family.

The introductory paragraph in this episode (6:1-2, 4a[b]b) explains the date and circumstances of the flood. It is distinguished from the preceding and following paragraphs by the cadence of long and short sentences, the sequence of consecutive and disjunctive clauses, and the repeated use of pronouns (*lāhem*, 6:1, 2, 4a[b]; *hēnnāh* 6:2; *hēmmāh*, 6:4b). The second paragraph begins and ends with what Yahweh sees (6:5, 8) and repeats that Yahweh regretted making man (6:6-7). The third has instructions for Noah that are repeated in observing his compliance (7:1a, 4, 7). The fourth describes the flood (7:17) but begins and ends with Noah safely in the ark (7:10, 16b, 23a[a]*b). The last paragraph is marked by intervals of seven days and the repeated release of the dove (8:6, 8-12). The story is complete with the final contrast between the increase of man and the decrease of water on the face of the earth (6:1a; 8:11).

The third episode is the story of Abraham. It is introduced by describing migrations from the east (Gen 11:2; cf. 2:8) and the gradual population of the whole world (11:1-7, 8b, 9b). It goes from the place of his birth to the birth of Isaac (12:1; 21:3) and explains how Abraham acquired the land of Canaan. The fourth is the story of Jacob. It is introduced by describing the migration of Isaac and relations with the Philistines (Gen 26:1a[a]b, 6-9, 11, 12-14, 16-17, 26-31) and continues with the migration of Jacob and his relations with Laban and Esau. Its boundaries are defined by patterns of recurrence in family life and in particular by the resolution of the conflict between Jacob and his brother.[18] The fifth episode is the story of Joseph. It is introduced as an example of agreement and conflict among the sons of Israel (Gen 37:3a, 4). It begins with the brothers tending their flocks in Shechem and Dothan and ends with them together with their flocks and herds in Egypt. The sixth is the story of Moses. It is introduced by describing the new regime in Egypt (Ex 1:8-11a, 12a, 22), continues with the details of Israel's exodus from Egypt, and ends with Balaam's blessing on the people that Yahweh brought out of Egypt. The whole narrative history ends as it began with Israel described as a garden free of enchantment (Num 23:23; 24:1) that Yahweh God planted by the water (Num 24:5-6).

The J narrative is remarkably terse. It is often abrupt, tends to insinuate and suggest, seems to presume familiarity with its material and leaves many things unexplained. It begins, for instance, with a sort of preterition that alludes to another story of creation that is left untold (Gen 2:4b-6). It suggests that Noah belonged to a race of giants that Yahweh destroyed (Gen 6:1-2, 4a[b]b) but it gives no indication what other wrong they might have done (Gen 6:5).[19] Abraham is not introduced but is presumed known (Gen 12:1). The narrative suggests but does not say that Lot and his family were killed in the destruction of Sodom and Gomorrah (Gen 19:12, 13a, 14).[20] Isaac is associated with Philistine settlement in the south, and Jacob is affiliated with the Aramaeans and situated in the north, but this is mentioned incidentally and the story in concerned mostly with family affairs. Jacob has twelve sons

(Gen 42:13, 32) and Joseph, Judah, Simeon, Benjamin and Levi are mentioned by name, but it is their relationship that is stressed and the names of the others and their tribal organization (Num 24:2) have no importance for the story. Moses acquired prestige and preeminence as the leader of his people but at the end of the story he simply disappears (cp. Num 20:14; 21:21). Instead of recounting how Israel took possession of the land the narrative closes with Balaam's visions of a settled people.

The J narrative, as these examples suggest, is a history and not simply a story. It is selective in its use of sources[21] and choice of materials,[22] deliberate in its organization[23] and manner of explanation,[24] purposeful and original in its interpretation.[25] It has the allusiveness that later commentaries were ready to dispel and the conciseness that subsequent versions were bound to elaborate.

Chapter 2

THE DTR^1 HISTORY

Noth defended his theory that there was only one Dtr author by attributing the secondary passages to later interpolators who wrote in the Dtr style but contributed nothing to the basic scheme of the history.[26] Revisions of his theory have tried to systematize this residue by assigning the secondary passages to one or two later editions of the history distinguished from each other by their language,[27] themes,[28] or interpretation.[29] This suppresses the anomaly in Noth's position, but it perpetuates his mistaken literary and historical assumptions and makes every Dtr the editor of received traditions rather than the author of a history. But, in fact, the complexity that Noth considered peripheral is original and integral to the history.[30] It is not due to editorial accretions or to the conglomeration of secondary passages but to Dtr^2's deliberate and systematic incorporation of an earlier version of the history (Dtr^1).

The Dtr^1 history is the sequel to J. It narrates the history of Israel from the last days of Moses to the reign of Hezekiah. Like J it is composed of episodes and paragraphs (Fig 2) and tells the story of heros and kings.[31] But it has more limited interests, and a narrower perspective, and is more clearly doctrinaire.

The history is based on a revision of the J Sinai covenant.[32] In the first episode (Fig 2: I, 1-16) Moses recalls the covenant at Horeb (par 1-2), the authority he received to interpret the covenant (par 3-4), and the promised conquest of the land (par 5-6).[33] He urges the people to observe the covenant (par 7-8), promulgates the law of centralization with its distinction between ritual and usual practice (par 9-10), lists the types of meat that can usually be eaten (par 11), and applies the law of centralization to the festivals of the Sinai covenant (par 12-14).[34] This first episode paraphrases the J covenant and makes centralization a corollary of the conquest.[35] It concludes by affirming the perpetual validity of the covenant (par 15) and by assuring Israel of the impending conquest (par 16).

The second episode is the story of the conquest under Joshua (Fig 2: II, 1-15). It begins by repeating assurances given in the first episode (par 1).[36] The reconnoitering of Jericho (par 2-5) confirms the gift of the land. Joshua makes a speech that repeats the gist of the Sinai convenant (par 6), and then the capture of Jericho and Ai illustrates the wonders that Yahweh announced (par 7-10).[37] The Gibeonites surrender (par 11-12), Joshua defeats the southern coalition led by Jerusalem and the northern coalition led by Hazor (par 13-14), and the conquest of the whole land takes place in accordance with the promise to Moses (par 15; Josh 11:23a[a] = 1:3b).

The covenant is observed in the annual pilgrimages by Elqanah and his family (Fig 2: III, 1-4) but then recedes until the end of the story. Its enduring validity is confirmed in the reign of Hezekiah when the law of centralization is enforced and Jerusalem is saved from the Assyrians by trust in Yahweh (Fig 2: VIII, 26-30). What intervenes is the history of the Davidic dynasty.

Dtr[1] wrote the history of Israel from the perspective of Judah and David. It mentions the northern kingdom only when it impinges on the affairs of Jerusalem and threatens the principles of centralization and dynastic succession that are entrenched in the covenant.

The history of the dynasty begins with the story of Samuel (Fig 2: III, 1-4), the reign of Saul (Fig 2: IV, 1-8), and the early career and accession of David (Fig 2: V, 1-11).[38] The next episode (Fig 2: VI, 1-6) opens with the promise to David that his son would succeed him (par 1) and then tells the story of the birth of Solomon (par 2-6). The seventh episode (Fig 2: VII, 1-17) recounts the disaffection and rebellion of Absalom. The eighth (Fig 2: VIII) begins with the revolt of Adonijah and the accession of Solomon (par 1-3) and traces the history of the Davidic dynasty to the reign of Hezekiah. It explains the secession of the northern kingdom (par 4-7) and its alienation from Jerusalem (par 8). It records the conflict of the early days (par 9-11), the settlement that was reached with Israel in the time of Jehoshaphat (par 12), and the circumstances of the interregnum under Athaliah (par 13-20). It describes the Aramaean threat to Jerusalem (par 21), attempts to overthrow the dynasty (par 22), corregency under Jotham (par 23-24), and the treaty with Tiglathpileser (par 25-26). The history ends with the fall of Samaria because it did not observe the covenant (par 27) and the deliverance of Jerusalem because it relied on Yahweh and rebelled against Assyria (par 28-30).[39]

The Dtr[1] history contains commentary (Fig 2: I, 1-6), legislation (Fig 2: I, 7-14), explanatory narratives (Fig 2: II, 1-5; III-VII), short descriptive accounts (Fig 2: II, 6-15; VIII, 13-20), and king-lists (Fig 2: VIII, 10-12, 21-25).[40] It is interested in negotiations and agreements. (Fig 2: I; II, 2-5, 11-12; V, 4-8; VI; VIII, 5-8, 25, 28-30), preoccupied with family affairs (Fig 2: II-V, VII), and fascinated by kings and war. It has literary resources such as J and Isaiah,[41] and favorite motifs such as battle reports (Fig 2: II, 5; VI, 5; VII, 14-16; VIII, 15-16), the influence of women on the course of events (Fig 2: II, 2-5; III, 1-4; VI, 1-6; VII, 1-8; VIII, 19-20) and the role of the king at the city gate (Fig 2: II, 2-3; IV, 4; VII, 9, 12, 15, 17). But it is mainly concerned with showing that the conquest took place in accordance with the covenant, and that the continued possession of the land was due to the Davidic dynasty and its unswerving dedication to the law of centralization. This original interpretation and obvious bias made it a profound and controversial history.

Chapter 3

THE P DOCUMENT

P was composed as an interpretation of J and as an alternative to Dtr[1].[42] It deletes the story of Joseph and rewrites the other episodes in J to demonstrate the ancient precedents for Israel's claim to the land.[43] It suppresses the Sinai covenant[44] and the theory of centralization that Dtr[1] combined with it, and replaces them with the promise to the patriarchs,[45] and with the sanctuary constructed on mount Sinai.[46]

P is both a complete and continuous history and a systematic commentary on J.[47] It is divided into five chapters that correspond to the episodes in J and that can be read either separately and sequentially or in combination with them (Fig 3).[48] It has lost the episodic character of the original and uses genealogies (Fig 3: II, 1; III, 1-7; IV, 1-2) and lists (Fig 3: V, 1-2) to smooth the transition between chapters.[49] It is combined with J in discrete segments to comment on the individual passages in their original sequence and has lost its own continuity in the new arrangement.

The first chapter (Gen 1:1-2:4a) gives the account of creation suggested but omitted in J's opening preterition (Gen 2:4b-6). It begins (1:1-2) and ends (1:31b-2:4a) with a summary of P's cosmology,[50] and is arranged in a triptych[51] that explains the beginning of time and of the calendar in order to dispel J's fascination with the origin of life and immortality. The first panel (Gen 1:1-12) describes the creation of the world and the origin of vegetation, but it preempts the J account by omitting the garden of Eden and the distinction between edible and forbidden fruit. The second panel (Gen 1:13-27) enlarges on the first by ordering and populating the world, but it eliminates the drama of the J narrative by confining man to a physical and generative hierarchy. The third panel (Gen 1:28-2:4a) expands on the first two, but corrects J's portrayal of the similarity between God and man by describing the dependence of living creatures on vegetation and by subordinating the created order to the festal calendar.[52]

The second chapter (Fig 3: II, 1-11) is a revision of the J flood story.[53] It eliminates divine collusion in the events leading to the flood by bracketing the innuendo in J (Gen 6: 1-2, 4a^{b}b-6, 7a^{a}b-8) with paragraphs that emphasize the sequence of human generations from Adam to Noah (par 1) and that blame the flood on the crimes of all living creatures (par 2).[54] It incorporates J's description of the flood into the covenant with Noah (par 3-4, 8-11), and then minimizes the flood by restricting it to a year in Noah's long life (Gen 7:11; 8:13a), by exempting a pair of all living creatures from its effect (par 5-7),[55] and by preserving the established order of creation.[56]

In the third chapter (Fig 3: III, 1-22) P uses the same device to comment on the J story of Abraham. It constructs an elaborate genealogy (par 1-7) to envelop and absorb J's story of the tower in Sumer and to correct J's confidence in human resourcefulness (Gen 11:1-7, 8b, 9b). It encloses J's story of Abraham and Lot in a date formula (par 8, 15) and changes J's promise of a son into a covenant concerning the land, posterity, and the worship of God (par 9-14).[57] It confirms the covenant, and comments on the story of Abraham's settlement by the oaks of Mamre (Gen 13:18a, J) by giving Abraham clear title to property in Hebron (par 16-21) and by having him buried there with Sarah (par 22).

The fourth chapter is the story of Jacob (Fig 3: IV, 1-8). It begins (par 1-2) with the genealogies of Ishmael and Isaac and ends with the genealogies of Esau and Jacob (par 6-8). It mitigates Jacob's deception of Isaac in J by noting in advance that Esau had sold Jacob his birthright (par 3), and by recalling later that Jacob returned to his father at Hebron and that he and Esau buried Isaac when he died (par 5). It omits the whole J narrative of Jacob's conflict with Esau and his sojourn in Haran, and interprets the account of Jacob's wrestling with God as a second apparition in which El Shaddai transferred to Israel the covenant with Abraham (par 4). It suppresses the Joseph story and simply relates that Jacob went to Egypt with his family and died there (par 6-8).[58]

In the fifth chapter (Fig 3: V, 1-43) P continues to use the same techniques to comment on J. After making a transition from the preceding chapter (par 1) it envelops the original J narrative in its own texts and then either ignores it, or replaces it, or rewrites it to suit its own interpretation. The most inclusive envelop establishes the credentials of Moses and Aaron (par 2-14) and then removes them from the scene (par 38-43). Within it another system of enclosure describes how the people of Israel lived (par 15-19) and died (par 34-37) in the wilderness. The third and central system contains the journey to Sinai and the instructions for building the sanctuary (par 20-25) and, with the construction of the sanctuary, the procedures for continuing on their journey (par 26-33). These three systems give the chapter a linear and periodic structure in which the segments are to be read sequentially, and a parabolic structure in which the segments are to be understood as sets of binary opposites.[59]

In the first segment (par 1-14) P begins with a summary of the sojourn in Egypt (par 1), alludes to the covenant with Noah (par 2; Exod 1:7 = Gen 1:28; 9:1), and absorbs J's introduction to the Sinai covenant in a reaffirmation of the covenant with Abraham, Isaac and Jacob (par 3). The central part of the segment replaces J's story of Moses' early life with an account of Yahweh's power and authority (par 4-10).[60] The segment closes with the instructions for the celebration of Passover in which P corrects the rules established by Dtr^{1} (par 11-13),[61] and then concludes with the chronology of the sojourn in Egypt (par 14).

In the second segment (par 15-19) P makes the victory at the sea, like the manna, a manifestation of the glory of Yahweh (Exod 14:4, 17-18; 16:7, 10). In the third segment (par 20-25) J's version of Yahweh's theophany on Sinai is replaced by the glory of Yahweh (Exod 24:15b-17) and by provision for the enduring presence of Yahweh in the sanctuary (Exod 29:43, 45-46). In the fourth, J's convenant on Sinai is replaced by the freewill offerings of the people and by the glory of Yahweh filling the sanctuary (par 26-33). The fifth segment (par 34-37) omits the intercession of Moses, the appeal to the Sinai covenant, and the example that J makes of Dathan and Abiram, and destroys the whole generation that despised the land. The last segment (par 38-43) obviously presupposes Dtr^1's account of the conquest under Joshua (Num 27:15-23; Deut 34:9) but it disagrees with Dtr^1's idea of the conquest and reaffirms that the land was promised to the patriarchs (Deut 34:4).

The importance of P is not only its disagreement with Dtr^1 and its alternative interpretation of J but the fact that it was one of the principal sources of Dtr^2's language and theology and the immediate inspiration for the revision of J undertaken by E.

Chapter 4

THE ELOHIST VERSION

E was composed as a supplement to J and P and as a preemptive variant to Dtr[1]. It contains four parts (Fig 4) that are individually complete and continuous but that were written for their separate contexts rather than in sequence to one another.[62] The first part (Fig 4: I, 1-11) was added after the J and P story of Abraham (Gen 10*-19*) and before the P account of the death of Abraham and Sarah (Gen 23:1-20; 25:7-10). It incorporates their version of the birth of Isaac (Gen 21:1-5) and elaborates on the circumstances of his birth and the events of his childhood. The second part (Fig 4: II, 1-16) was inserted into the P story of Jacob's journey to Paddan Aram (Gen 28:1-5; 35:9-13, 15) and was interwoven with the J history of Jacob and Laban (Gen 29*-33*). It describes Jacob's encounter with God at Bethel (par 1-3, 13-16) and introduces an elaborate illustration of divine providence (par 4-12). The third part contains a variant to the Joseph story narrated by J (Fig 4: III, 1-30) and an expansion on the notice of Jacob's death recorded in P (Fig 4: III, 31-37). It is either combined with J (par 1-8, 25-30) or inserted into it (par 9-24). Its inclusion separates P from J and makes P seem less like a commentary on J than a framework to the composite narrative. The last part (Fig 4: IV, 1-36) is an alternative to the J and P accounts of Sinai and a response to the Dtr[1] implementation of J's Sinai covenant. It follows J and P in recounting that Moses encountered God (par 1-2), and follows Dtr[1] in locating the encounter at Horeb (Exod 3:1; cf. Deut 5:2), but it differs from all these sources in omitting the land and the assurance that Israel would possess it. It agrees with J and P in describing the exodus as a great victory (par 3-5) but it changes the emphasis of the story by adding a sequel on the authority of Moses and the administration of justice (par 6-10). It replaces J's Sinai covenant and P's account of the sanctuary with the revelation of the law (par 11-30), rejects Dtr[1]'s synthesis of covenant, conquest and centralization in favor of special divine providence (par 31-32), and is more conciliatory than Dtr[1] in explaining the defection of the northern kingdom (par 33-35). It ends when Moses has finished speaking to the people and covers his face (par 36).

In E, as in the other sources, each part comprises grammatically distinct paragraphs that give the narrative its structure and coherence. Continuous narrative is marked by paragraphs that begin consecutively and end disjunctively.[63] Paragraphs that begin and end consecutively indicate the end of a story or incident.[64] Paragraphs that begin disjunctively and end consecutively are summaries.[65] Those that begin and end disjunctively are new beginnings or emphatic transitions in the narrative.[66] Paragraphs that begin with *wyhy* introduce incidents that are related chronologically or thematically to the topic of a prior but not immediately preceding paragraph.[67]

In the first part, for instance, the agreement between Abraham and Abimelek (Fig 4: I, 1-3) and the banishment of Ishmael (par 4-6) are two distinct stories: their opening paragraphs begin consecutively and end disjunctively, but their final paragraphs begin and end consecutively to mark the close of the narrative (par 3, 6). The next incident records the treaty between Abraham and Abimelek (par 7-8): it is introduced by *wyhy* to indicate that it continues the story of their earlier agreement (par 1-3) rather than the preceding story of the banishment of Ishmael. The final incident is the sacrifice of Isaac (par 9-11): it is introduced by *wyhy* since it supposes the exclusion of Ishmael and is not related directly to the treaty between Abraham and Abimelek that immediately precedes it. The middle paragraph in this incident (par 10) begins and ends disjunctively because it is the turning-point in the story and emphasizes E's confidence in divine providence.

This system of paragraphing distinguishes the incidents in each part and relates them to each other both serially and analogically. For instance, the first and third incidents situate Abraham in the Negeb (par 1-3, 7-8), and the second and fourth incidents dispose of his children (par 4-6, 9-11). But there is also a serial logic since the first and second incidents cast doubt on the paternity of Isaac (par 1-6), but the third and fourth reaffirm divine providence in the choice of Abraham and his progeny (par 7-11).

The second part has the same system of paragraphing and a similar structure and coherence.[68] There are four incidents related to each other both sequentially and analogically. The first recounts Jacob's dream at Bethel (Fig 4: II, 1-3) and is balanced by the fourth in which Jacob meets the angels of God and returns to Bethel (par 13-16). The second incident repeats J (Gen 30:25-42) and explains how Jacob outwitted Laban with the help of divine providence (par 4-8). It is balanced by the third that reiterates divine providence in Jacob's escape from Paddan Aram and his treaty with the Aramaeans (par 9-12).[69] But the incidents are also consecutive and gradually fulfill the conditions of Jacob's vow by describing how God was with him (par 1-8: cf. Gen 31:5) and took care of him on his journey (par 9-16; cf. Gen 35:1, 6-7).

This style and organization enable E to construct a version of the history that is both a continuous narrative and a commentary on the text it supplements. The third part (Fig 4: III, 1-37), for instance, is a different version of the Joseph story that comments on J and supplies for the omissions in P. The first incident (par 1-7) corrects most of the details in J and relates how Joseph was brought to Egypt. The second (par 8-21) differs from J by describing how Joseph lost favor with Potiphar but by the grace of God became the ruler of the land of Egypt. The third (par 22-30) continues the story but also resumes the first incident and explains that the sojourn was providential for the whole nation. The fourth (par 31-37) completes the story but also refers to the second incident and explains how Joseph acquired preeminence among his brothers.

Similarly, the fourth part (Fig 4: IV, 1-36) contains three incidents that constitute a complete and continuous narrative but that are arranged as a commentary on the earlier versions. The exodus leads to worship on the mountain (par 1-6) and is contrasted with the rebellion of the people and the worship of the golden calf (par 33-36). These two incidents give prominence to the third (par 7-32) in which E substitutes the law and divine providence for the covenant on Sinai proclaimed by J, for the exclusiveness supported by Dtr[1], and for the assurance of God's presence defended by P.

Its style and organization indicate that E is not a traditional variant of J[70] but an original composition written to supplement and revise J and its congeners. This appreciation is supported by the historical evidence that E used J, P and Dtr^1 as sources for its own interpretation.

In the first part E applies to Abraham two stories that J told of Isaac (Fig 4: I, 1-3, 7-8; cp. Fig 1: IV, 1-4), combines them with information from P on the expulsion of Ishmael (Fig 4: I, 4-6; cp. Fig 3: III, 9, 13-14), and borrows the theory of centralization from Dtr^1 for its story of the sacrifice of Isaac (Fig 4: I, 9-11; cp. Fig 2: I, 9). In the second part E relies on J for the story of Jacob's journey (Fig 4: II, 4-6, 14-17; cp. Fig 1: IV, 12-19), on P for the story of divine revelation at Bethel (Fig 4: II, 1-3; cp. Fig 3: IV, 4), and on Dtr^1 for the idea that vows and tithes are to be paid at the central sanctuary (Fig 4: II, 1-3, 17; cp. Fig 2: I, 10, 12). In the third part E follows J in developing the story of Joseph, and P in elaborating the circumstances of Jacob's death, but rewrites these sources to give precedence to the tribes of Joseph. In the fourth part E agrees with J in describing the exodus (Fig 4: IV, 1-6; cp. Fig 1: VI, 5-10), with P in alluding to a time of conflict in the wilderness (fig 4: IV, 7-10; cp. Fig 3: V, 18-19), and with Dtr^1 in contrasting the idea of a central sanctuary and the construction of the golden calves (Fig 4: IV, 31-36; cp. Fig 2: VIII, 4-8), but it completely changes these sources by incorporating the revelation of the law.

E is particularly interested in the issues affecting the northern kingdom. It displaces Abraham from Hebron and the sphere of Judaean influence to Beersheba and the realm of the Philistines. It is aware of the law of centralization and juxtaposes the conflicting claims of Bethel and the mountain in the land of Moriah (Fig 4: I, 9-11; II, 1-3). It alludes to the struggles with the Aramaeans in Gilead (Fig 4: II, 7-13) and has Jacob travel through the major royal cities of the northern kingdom (Fig 4: II, 14-17). It distinguishes Joseph among his brothers and gives the blessing of Israel to Ephraim and Manasseh (Fig 4: III, 29-35). It uses the name "God" and corrects the emphasis that P gave to the name "Yahweh" by making it a studied variant (Fig 4: IV, 1-6). It abandons the theory of a complete and marvelous conquest propounded by J and Dtr^{1} and proposes instead a distinctive law and the assurance of gradual possession of the land.

E, like P, was an important source of ideas and language for Dtr^{2}. In particular its potential appeal to a northern audience allowed Dtr^{2} to rewrite the sources as a history of the twelve tribes of Israel.

Chapter 5

THE DTR^2 HISTORY

The Dtr^2 history is a comprehensive and systematic revision of the sources. It continues the process of interpretation initiated by Dtr^1 and developed by P and E. But it is neither a source nor a separate and continuous work. It is rather a running commentary on the sources, distinguished from them by its language, style, organization and interests.

I. Organization

A principal feature of the Dtr^2 interpretation is its reorganization of the sources. The Dtr^2 history is composed of books, parts and chapters that incorporate the sources and preserve their original segmentation, but that also redistribute the segments in a new system of reference. This system combines the principles of periodicity and polar opposition that were used by P with a developed form of the argument from analogy that was introduced by E. It allows Dtr^2 to homogenize the sources and integrate them into a complete and continuous history (Fig 5).

A. The books correspond generally to the order of the printed Bible. The first book is Genesis. It comprises seven parts that are related to each other both serially and analogically, marshalling events in logical and chronological sequence and also explaining their relationship to each other.

1. The first part (Fig 5: I, A, 1-4), for example, records the J and P stories of creation but adds conflict and crime (Gen 4:1-26), curse and banishment (Gen 3:14-19). It leads into the next part by describing the circumstances that justify the flood, but it is also balanced and explained by the seventh part that contains all its polar opposites (Fig 5: I, G, 1-5): in the conclusion to the Joseph story crime is replaced by forgiveness, conflict by reconciliation, curse by the blessing of Jacob, and banishment by prosperous settlement in Egypt.[71]

2. Dtr^2's penchant for argumentation and explanation is also evident in the organization of the other parts. The second part (Fig 5: I, B, 1-5), for instance, contains the J and P flood story and Dtr^2 additions pertaining to the aboriginal inhabitants of the world and to the origin of legitimate sacrifice. In its Dtr^2 version it is explicitly the sequel to the story of creation (Gen 5:29b^b). But it is also a partial analogue to the story of Joseph (Fig 5: I, F, 1-10): in both stories the hero's rescue anticipates the survival of a small and exclusive group; in both there is a Canaanite interlude in which an ancestor of this group achieves notoriety (B, 5; F, 3); in both the shedding of blood is prohibited (B, 5; F, 2); and in both the preservation of life is ascribed to the immediate intervention of God on behalf of the hero (B, 1-5; F, 4, 10). This use of periodicity and analogy gives force to the argument and coherence to the history: the fact that the world was filled with violence and was destroyed by a flood acquires immediacy in the crime of Joseph's brothers and the ensuing world famine; the example of Noah and Joseph in separate times and disparate circumstances is an argument for the continuance of divine providence and a reason to expect another hero in the next calamity.

3. The third and fifth parts (Fig 5: I, C, 1-5; E, 1-11) compose another set of symmetrical opposites, both contributing to the continuous history and also rationalizing its development. The fifth part tells the story of Isaac whose birth was the point of the fourth part; the third part concludes the Mesopotamian phase of the history that began in the garden of Eden (Gen 2:10-14). But both parts are filled with elements that are tangential to the chronological and narrative sequence and contribute to the system of interpretation. The most obvious is the story of Abraham in Egypt that was composed to balance and explain the story of Isaac among the Philistines (C, 3 = E, 1). Similarly, the blessings declared to Abraham (Gen 12:2-3) are portrayed in the life of Jacob (E, 1-3, 10). Or, again, Abraham travels from Shechem to Bethel to Hebron (C, 3) and Jacob follows the same route (E, 8-10). Abraham inaugurates the construction of altars and the invocation of Yahweh (C, 3-4) that becomes a convention in the days of Isaac

and Jacob (E, 1, 8, 10). The promise of the land and descendants (C, 4) has a sort of fulfillment in the time of Jacob (E, 4-6) but, like the expectation of universal blessing, or the circuit of royal cities, it is not specific to either story but is part of the overlapping interpretation that gives the history uniformity and purpose.

4. The logic of Dtr^2's reorganization of the sources is particularly evident in the fourth part (Fig 5: I, D, 1-11; Gen 15-24). J's story of Abraham told of migrations from the east, the travels of Abraham and Lot, the destruction of Sodom and Gomorrah, Abraham's tranquil possession of the land, and the birth of Sarah's son. P's commentary had already fragmented the story by adding genealogies, inserting the story of Ishmael, conceptualizing the promise of a son, and appending references to the death and burial of Abraham and Sarah. The E version, finally, disagreed with the thrust of the J narrative and approved the P notion of covenant and promise by relating incidents that cast doubt on Isaac's lineage and made him Abraham's heir by divine intervention. But then Dtr^2 took the story and its interpretations and divided them into two parts. One part (Fig 5: I, C, 1-5; Gen 10-14) emphasized Abraham's role in world history by describing his relations with Egypt and Mesopotamia.[72] But the other part (Fig 5: I, D, 1-11) contains a synthesis of Dtr^2's ideas and a proleptic summary of the ensuing history. It begins with an historical synthesis that does not pertain to the present story but explains the significance of Abraham and the promise for the generations to come (Gen 15).[73] It contains reflections on the life of Abraham and the relationship between divine guidance, the observance of the law, and the fulfillment of the promises (D, 4, 6, 8, 10). It makes prophecy the standard of interpretation by revealing the future to Abraham in dreams, visions and oracles, and by referring the promises and blessings to prophetic instruction and intercession (D, 1, 4, 6). Its principal function is to formulate Dtr^2's theory of history and the rules of interpretation that are observed in the following chapters and books.

5. The system that pertains in the organization of the book also governs the arrangement of chapters in each part and

the relationship of paragraphs in the individual chapters. It is a logical order with formal literary aspects that can be abstracted and schematized (for instance, ABB'A' and its variants), and with historical aspects that depend on the peculiar interplay of text and repeated interpretation.

For example, the third part (Gen 10-14) contains five chapters symmetrically arranged. The first chapter (Gen 10) gives ethnographic data on the peoples, nations and cities that are at war in the last chapter (Gen 14). The second and fourth chapters (Gen 11, 13) narrate the dispersal of peoples and the inhabitation of the world. The middle chapter (Gen 12) is asymmetrical and introduces themes that are developed in the rest of the book. However, the historical significance of this part does not consist only in its formal arrangement but in the cumulative effect of text and commentary. The ethnographic data, for instance, is a revision of the genealogy that P constructed (Fig 3: III, 1-7) to correct J's interpretation of the origin of nations (Gen 11:1-7, 8b, 9b). It acquires an extended meaning in the program of universal blessing (Gen 12:2-3), the anticipation of the exodus (Gen 12:10-20), and the description of the promised land (Gen 13:14-17) that Dtr^2 inserted into J's story of Abraham's settlement in Canaan. And it acquires an instructive or parabolic significance in the concluding story of Abraham's alliance with Sodom and Gomorrah against Babylon and the nations (Gen 14).

The paragraph arrangement of the individual chapters illustrates the same literary and historical method. The Abraham covenant (Gen 15), for example, is composed of four paragraphs ordered symmetrically. The first and fourth are concerned with Abraham's offspring and their inheritance (Gen 15:1-5, 17-21), the second and third with the correspondence between Abraham's exodus from Ur of the Chaldaeans and the exodus of his descendants from an alien land (Gen 15:6-11, 12-16). Similarly, the first and third paragraphs portray Abraham as a prophet and describe his prophetic vision, and the second and fourth define the covenant and its conditions. But the historical significance of the covenant consists not only in its formal arrangement but in its position in the complex system of reference constructed by Dtr^2.

B. The second book, Exodus, has seven parts (Fig 5: II, A-G). The first part (Exod 1-5) contains J's narrative of the early life of Moses and his encounters with Yahweh, P's summary of Egyptian oppression, and E's version of the assurance that Moses received. Dtr^2 reorganized the narrative and its interpretations by including a different story of Miriam, Moses and Aaron (A, 2-4), and by enclosing it in another version of Egyptian oppression that describes the building of royal store cities by Israelite slave labor (A, 1, 5). The second part (Exod 6-12) elaborates on P's plague narrative with another version of the plagues that illustrates the distinctiveness of Israel and defines the intercessory role cf Moses (Exod 7-11). Then it encloses this revised version between the Levitical genealogy of Moses and Aaron and the rituals for Unleavened Bread and the offering of the first-born (B, 1, 7).[74] The third part (Exod 13-18) contains the victory over the Egyptians related by all the sources, the wilderness itinerary and the gift of the manna recorded by P, and the rules for the administration of justice outlined by E. The Dtr^2 version enclosed the victory in a system of rebellion and holy war (C, 2, 5 = Exod 14, 17), included Miriam, and added exhortations to observe the law and the sabbath (C, 3-4 = Exod 15-16). Then Dtr^2 enveloped the complete history in legislation that memorialized the exodus (C, 1, 6 = Exod 13, 18). The fourth and central part contains the theophany on Sinai and the revelation of the law (Exod 19-24). Dtr^2 inserted the decalogue and related materials (D, 2-5) and enclosed them in the covenant ritual and ceremonial vision of God (D, 1, 6). The fifth part (Exod 25-31) contains the instructions that P gave for the building of the sanctuary. Dtr^2 inserted the ritual for the ordination of Aaron (Exod 27-29) and enclosed it with plans for the construction of the tent of meeting (E, 1-2, 6-7 - Exod 25-26, 30-31). The sixth part contains E's story of the golden calf and J's narrative of the covenant on Sinai (F, 1-3). Dtr^2 inserted a compendium on guidance in the wilderness and the distinctiveness of Israel (F, 2 = Exod 33), and then enclosed it in a revision of J and E that emphasized the intercessory role of Moses, the fidelity of the Levites, and the rituals pertaining to the offering of the first-born (F, 1, 3 = Exod 32, 34). The last part contains the P account of the building of the sanctuary (Exod 35-40). Dtr^2 inserted the construction of all the ritual paraphernalia and the preparations for the ordination of Aaron (G, 3-4 = Exod 37-38), and enclosed it in a revision of P that turned the sanctuary into the tent of meeting (G, 1-2, 5-6 = Exod 35-36, 39-40).

The system of enclosure that the book of Exodus uses to reorganize and interpret the sources illustrates Dtr^2's perception of history.[75] Everything has its match, parallel, opposite, or other side, and history consists in the sets of interrelationships that can be discerned among them. The relationships can be serial and sequential: the book of Exodus is part of a story that tells how Israel went from slavery and forced labor in Egypt to volunteer labor and freewill offerings on Sinai. The relationships can also be complementary and contrastive: the objective of the journey from Egypt to Sinai is the worship of Yahweh (Fig 5: II, A-G), but there is a parallel longing for servitude in Egypt that leads to the worship of the golden calf (Fig 5: II, C, F). The relationships can also be merely logical: the difference between servitude and service is marked by the sabbath, and repeated exhortations to observe it create an artificial link in the story (C, 4; D, 2, 5; E, 7; F, 3; G, 1). The relationships can be analogical: the sabbath is the sign of the Sinai covenant (Exod 31:12-17) as circumcision was the sign of the covenant with Abraham; their analogical relationship is expressed by including the exodus in the promise to the patriarchs (Gen 15:12-16) and, conversely, by making the promises to Abraham contingent on the observance of the law (Gen 18:19; 22:18; 26:2-5). Finally, the relationships can be metaphorical: the sabbath is a metaphor of creation (Exod 20:8-11) and the injunctions to observe it that are associated with the building of the sanctuary (Exod 31:12-17; 35:1-3) suggest a complementarity of creation and the dwelling place of God that becomes explicit in Dtr^2's consideration of the Solomonic temple (I Kgs 8).

C. The third book has six parts (Fig 5: III, A-F) and is mainly a Dtr^2 composition.

1. The first part (A, 1-4) completes the observances that were prescribed on Sinai and comprises four chapters arranged in symmetrical order. The first chapter (Lev 8:1-36)

describes the consecration of Aaron and his sons and the eating of the ordination sacrifice, and the fourth (Lev 11:1-45) prescribes dietary rules to ensure the holiness of the people. The second chapter (Lev 9:1-24) contains sacrificial rituals and the third (Lev 10:1-20) is linked to it artificially both by mention of the fire that comes from Yahweh (Lev 9:22-24 = 10:1-3) and by renewed discussion of the same rituals (Lev 10: 12-20).

2. The second part (B, 1-10) describes the organization of the twelve tribes of Israel around the tent of meeting. Its chapters are arranged symmetrically, as usual, and portray the organization of the camp from its outer perimeter into the central position occupied by the tabernacle. The first two chapters (Num 1-2) record a census of the tribes and describe their axial position around the tent of meeting, and the last two chapters (Num 9-10) repeat the same information in describing the order of march. The inside chapters (Num 3-4, 7-8) assign the Levites a place around the tabernacle and explain their rights and duties in pitching and transporting the tent of meeting. The middle chapters (Num 5-6) describe the priestly functions of Aaron and his sons who minister before Yahweh. As the concentric arrangement of the chapters corresponds to the zones of exclusion in the camp, so their logical sequence describes the gradual preparations for its journey from Sinai. The combined serial and analogical order of the chapters explains how the twelve tribes became the congregation that marched victoriously through the wilderness.

3. The third part (C, 1-9) is a reasoned account of rebellion in the wilderness and refusal of the promised land. Its central chapter (Num 15) looks ahead to the rituals and practices to be observed in the land, and looks back on an incident that occurred in the wilderness. This prospect and retrospect is enclosed by two chapters (Num 14, 16) that contain the J and P story of rebellion in the wilderness and Dtr[2]'s revision proving that only the guilty were punished. This story is enclosed between two chapters (Num 13, 17) that recount the antecedent and sequel to the rebellion: the first is the scout narrative (Num 13), the second explains why Aaron is the leader of the tribe of Levi (Num 17), and the two are

related artificially by repeated use of the same word in different senses (*maṭṭeh* = "rod, tribe"). Finally, the complete account is enclosed by two chapters (Num 12, 18) that delimit the functions of Aaron and the Levites at the tent of meeting, and then by two others (Num 11, 19) that are concerned with the boundaries of the camp. This analogical arrangement of the chapters reflects the concentric organization of the camp, from its environs (Num 11-12, 18-19), through the tribal muster on its periphery (Num 13, 17), to the tent of meeting (Num 14, 16) and the central place of sacrifice (Num 15). But the linear and logical sequence of the chapters reflects the order of march, with Moses and the tent of meeting outside the camp, and describes the hierarchy of prophets, priests, and Levites, heads of tribes, elders and leaders. The two systems combine to represent Dtr^2's thinking on the religious and political organization of the tribes.

4. The fourth part (D, 1-6) is the converse of the third and describes the rebellions of Moses and Aaron and Israel's victories in Transjordan. The first chapter (Num 20) has J's story of the embassy to Edom that P combined with the story of Meribah and the death of Aaron. Dtr^2 added the death of Miriam (20:1b), Yahweh's disclosure to Moses and Aaron at the tent of meeting (20:6), the beginning of Israel's circuitous route through Transjordan (20:19-21), and the idea of priestly succession (20:26, $28a^a$). The second chapter (Num 21) is J's story of the embassy to Sihon and Israel's victory over the Amorites. Dtr^2 turned it into a victory over Sihon and Og (21:25-35), added renewed rebellion (21:4b-9), and made it part of the Transjordanian itinerary (21:10-20). The third chapter (Num 22) is J's story of Balak's embassy to Balaam. Dtr^2 described the embassy and added the story of Balaam's ass that ridiculed divination and contrasted it with the orthodox theory of divine inspiration. The fourth chapter (Num 23) is J's story of Balaam's oracles and the vision of a settled people. Dtr^2 added cross-references to the theory of prophecy, to the patriarchal promises, and to the expectation of a victorious king. The fifth chapter (Num 24) concludes the J narrative with another of Balaam's oracles and his dismissal, but the Dtr^2 version continues its exposition of prophecy and develops

its allusions to the victorious king with a collection of sayings against the nations. The last chapter (Num 25) is Dtr^2's story of the revolt at Baal Peor and the succession of the Aaronide Phinehas to the priesthood.

Dtr^2's systematic interpretation gradually relativized the J narrative by making the defeat of the Amorites a stage in the detour through Transjordan, by turning Balaam's vision into a prophecy concerning a future king's defeat of the nations, and by combining this prophecy with the promise of priestly succession. The revision follows the usual method of argumentation and produces the familiar pattern of concentric recurrence. Dtr^2 begins by gathering information on the rebellion of Aaron (Num 20), the defeat of Sihon and Og (Num 21), and the difference between prophecy and divination (Num 22). Then Dtr^2 draws the conclusion that Balaam was a prophet (Num 23), includes a prophecy on the future king's defeat of the nations (Num 24), and concludes a perpetual covenant with the Aaronide priesthood (Num 25).

5. The fifth part (E, 1-6) describes tribal organization in Transjordan. It is the analogue of the second part (Num 1-10) and is linked to it in some obvious ways. The first chapter (Num 26) is a census of the tribes that balances the census at Sinai (Num 1), refers to it (Num 26:61, 64 = Num 1:3; 3:4), and has the same conscriptional purpose (Num 1:3; 26:2). The last chapter (Num 31) illustrates this purpose in the Midianite war and also duplicates the offerings for the Levites and the tabernacle that were described in the corresponding second part (Num 31:21-54; Num 7). The second chapter (Num 27) prefaces P's story of the succession of Joshua with a discussion of the inheritance of the daughters of Zelophehad. It is balanced by the fifth chapter (Num 30) that legislates women's dependence on men in the matter of vows, and both are parallel to the discussion of women and vows in the corresponding second part (Num 5-6). The third and fourth chapters (Num 28-29) list the offerings and yearly festivals. They suppose the ritual order that was established in the corresponding part (Num 9-10) and refer specifically to its prescriptions for the celebration of Passover and the blowing of trumpets (Num 9:1-14; 10:10).

6. The last part of the book (F, 1-5) describes the role

of the Transjordanian tribes in the allottment of inheritances and summarizes the history of Israel from Egypt to the borders of the land. It is connected with the corresponding first part (Lev 8-11) particularly by its references to Eleazar (Lev 10:6, 12, 16; Num 34:17) and to the anointing of the high priest (Lev 8:12; Num 35:25). In the first chapter (Num 32) the Transjordanian tribes are reminded of Israel's rejection of the land, are designated the vanguard in the conquest of Canaan, and receive the captured kingdoms of Sihon and Og. In the second (Num 33) a list of stations in the wilderness is the occasion for reviewing the events as far as the plains of Moab at the Jordan near Jericho. The third chapter (Num 34) makes the point of the prospect and review in these chapters by describing the borders of Canaan and naming the tribal leaders who will assist in its apportionment. The fourth chapter (Num 35) continues the same topic by assigning the Levitical cities but is also attached to the second chapter by its location in the plains of Moab at the Jordan near Jericho and by its reference to the proportionality between the size of a tribe and the extent of its inheritance (Num 33:54; 35:8). The last chapter (Num 36) returns to the subject of the Transjordanian tribes and amends the ruling that was given in the case of the case of the daughters of Zelophehad in order to maintain the integrity and distinctiveness of all the tribes.

D. The fourth book, Deuteronomy, reflects on all the preceding history and legislation (Fig 5: IV, A-F). It rationalizes the impending conquest and incorporates the Dtr^1 covenant in a system of interpretation that gives it an entirely different meaning.[76] This system is evident in its organization. There is a comprehensive historical framework (Deut 1-3, 31-34) that relates the rebellions of the past to the future defections in the land. It envelops a didactic legal framework (Deut 4-11, 26-30) that describes the treaty between Yahweh and Israel and the consequences of violating it. Both enclose a systematic presentation of the law from the perspective of the community (Deut 12-18) and its individual members (Deut 19-25).

1. The first part (Deut 1-3) is a Dtr^2 composition that quotes from the earlier books and contrasts the refusal of the

land by the wilderness generation with the conquest of Transjordan by the following generation. The last part (Deut 31-34) complements it by expanding P's record of the death of Moses into an anticipation of the conquest and a prediction of subsequent rebellion. The two are related sequentially, since together they summarize the entire history of the nation, and analogically, since the first is explicitly the model for the second (e.g. Deut 1:37-38; 31:4, 27).

2. The second part (Deut 4-11) incorporates the Dtr^1 version of J's Sinai covenant into a commentary on the decalogue. Dtr^2 argues that the covenant is the decalogue (Deut 4) and that its observance is required for the possession of the land (Deut 11). This argument is illustrated by two opposite interpretations of the revelation on Horeb, one that relates the observance of the decalogue and the possession of the land (Deut 5-6), the other that relates the worship of the golden calf and the loss of the land (Deut 9-10). The argument is reinforced by showing that the decalogue is what distinguishes Israel from the nations (Deut 7) and by warning that its neglect will condemn Israel to their fate (Deut 8).

In this part Dtr^2 repeats as a commentary on Dtr^1 what the earlier books had included as a revision of J. The result of this duplication is a systematic and coherent interpretation and a progressively more comprehensive homogenization of the sources. What Dtr^2 meant independently of these sources is expressed in the corresponding fifth part (Deut 26-30) that contrasts the curses attendant on disregard for the covenant with the blessings that follow obedience to the law.

3. The third part (Deut 12-18) subsumes Dtr^1's centralization of worship under a theory of community organization. Dtr^1 distinguished between offering sacrifice and eating meat, determined when sacrifice should be offered at the central sanctuary, and listed what meat could be eaten. Dtr^2 included these innovations in a legislative system that was designed to eliminate the worship of other gods. The first chapter (Deut 12) agrees that meat can be eaten anywhere, but makes it a sacrifice and an exception to the rule, and considers that the central sanctuary and its rituals are a means of extirpating the worship of other gods. The last chapter (Deut 18) continues the same theme by listing the portions of a sacrifice

that belong to the Levitical priests, and by making prophecy the antidote to divination and the abominable practices of the nations. The second and sixth chapters (Deut 13, 17) create the courts and determine the procedures to be followed in cases of sedition, and the third and fifth chapters (Deut 14, 16) enumerate the sacrificial animals and list the festivals to be observed at the central sanctuary. The fourth chapter (Deut 15) has no complement or polar opposite. It describes the social and economic order that distinguishes Israel from the nations and emphasizes the distinctiveness of Israel that is presupposed by all the surrounding legislation.

4. The fourth part (Deut 19-25) is mainly a revision of the legislation that E introduced into the covenant at Sinai. It defines particular aspects of community organization and has the usual symmetrical and explanatory order.[77]

The first chapter (Deut 19) contains legislation on blood vengeance, boundary stones and witnesses, and is held together by a system of cross-references: the first and second laws mention borders and the occupation of hereditary land (Deut 19:8-10, 14), and the first and third have the same formula excluding leniency (Deut 19:13, 21). The last chapter (Deut 25) has laws concerning the administration of justice (Deut 25:1-4, 11-16), levirate marriage, and the extermination of the Amalekites (Deut 25:5-10, 17-19) and is bound together by the same system of cross-reference: the administration of justice is governed by a concern for equity and proportion (*ṣdq* 25:1, 15), and the rules on levirate marriage and war with Amalek are both concerned with the blotting out of a name (*mḥh šm // zkr*, 25:6, 19). But these two chapters are also complementary and both logically and analogically interrelated: both contain laws that reserve punishment to the discretion of the court; both are concerned with the destruction of the nations, the inheritance of the land, the observance of the law and the dangers of long journeys; both resolve issues that affect the principles of inheritance but are beyond the jurisdiction of the courts and anomalous in a legal system that forbids murder and adultery.

This systematization of the laws is also evident in the serial and analogical relationship of the other chapters. The second and sixth chapters (Deut 20, 24) contain similar exemptions from battle and legislate the treatment of women, children, slaves, sojourners and property in times of war and peace. The third and fifth chapters (Deut 21, 23) are concerned with the integrity of the land and the camp, with the treatment of aliens, and with the succession of generations. The middle chapter (Deut 22) contains laws of property that are associated by their mention of domestic animals, clothing, and chance occurrence. It refers explicitly to the first chapter for one of its precedents (Deut 19:11; 22:26) and is connected in various ways with the other chapters: it uses the example of house, vineyard and wife on which exemptions were based in the second chapter (Deut 20:5-7; 22:8, 9, 13); it supposes the distinction that was made in the third chapter between what happens in the city and what happens in the open country (Deut 21:1-9; 22:23, 25); it mentions the notions of holiness and abomination that recur in the fifth chapter (22:5, 9; 23:15, 18-19), the question of divorce that is treated in the sixth chapter (22:13-21; 24:1-4), and the building of a house that is used metaphorically in the last chapter (22:8; 25:9).

E. The fifth book, Joshua, is a reinterpretation of the Dtr^1 story of the conquest (Fig 5: V, A-C).[78] It is the periodic opposite of the book of Deuteronomy, demonstrating the validity of the covenant in the occupation and allottment of the land, and it is the sequel to the book of Leviticus-Numbers, describing the conquest that was refused by the wilderness generation and then meticulously prepared in Transjordan. With Deuteronomy it is the turning-point in the Dtr^2 history, synthesizing the past and devising a program for the future. The earlier books assemble the elements that are crucial to their interpretation, such as the promise to the patriarchs, the law and the covenant, and the formation of the wilderness community. The following books illustrate their understanding of history and retrace their themes.[79]

1. The first part (Josh 1-8) has the Dtr^1 narrative of the capture of Jericho and Ai but rewrites it to prove that the conquest took place in obedience to the law of Moses. The rewriting consists in adding opposites and rearranging the earlier version. Dtr^1's story of the spies is matched by Dtr^2's commission to the Transjordanian vanguard (Josh 1:12-18): the spies

become redundant and their story becomes an occasion for Rahab's confession of faith. Dtr^1 introduced the conquest of Jericho with a speech of Joshua before crossing the Jordan (Josh 3:5, 10b) but Dtr^2 changed the speech (Josh 3:1-5, 9-13), added others to suppress it (Josh 3:6-8, 14-17), and made the crossing of the Jordan a detailed doublet of the crossing of the Red Sea (Josh 3-4). Dtr^1 considered the conquest of Jericho one of the wonders of Yahweh, but Dtr^2 combined it with the theory of the ban, modeled it on Israel's journey through the wilderness, and turned it into a triumphant procession (Josh 5-6). Dtr^1's story of the conquest of Ai was preempted by Dtr^2's duplicate story of sin and defeat (Josh 7), was rewritten to resemble the defeat of Amalek under Moses (Josh 8:18), and was enclosed in a ritual and symbolic occupation of the land (Josh 7-8).

This method of composition facilitates the incorporation of disparate and even contradictory opinions, and contributes to the development of intricate and sophisticated argumentation. The four pairs of opposites (Josh 1-2, 3-4, 5-6, 7-8) have complex sets of relationships: they combine text and commentary, follow each other sequentially, and interpret each other analogically. For instance, the first pair (Josh 1-2) combines a Dtr^1 text in which Joshua is the successor of Moses with a Dtr^2 commentary in which Joshua is a new Moses. It also mentions the crossing of the Red Sea (2:10) that becomes the topic of the next pair (Josh 3-4), the rescue of Rahab and her family (2:12-14) that is an issue in the third pair (Josh 5-6), and the possibility of an exception to the ban (2:15-21) that is discussed in the fourth pair (Josh 7-8). But it is also the analogue of the fourth pair since both contain deception, an attempt to assimilate Joshua to Moses, and an interest in the book of the law.

2. The second part (Josh 9-11) incorporates the Dtr^1 narrative of the conquest in a disquisition on the theory of the ban. The first chapter (Josh 9) refers to the earlier legislation on war and treaties (Deut 7, 20), but it exonerates Joshua by blaming the leaders for the treaty with Gibeon, and by reducing the Gibeonites to the status of slaves. The second chapter (Josh 10) illustrates the proper procedure for

implementing the ban, and the third (Josh 11) claims that the ban was observed against all the cities except Gibeon.

3. The third part (Josh 12-24) reconsiders the conquest from the perspective of the individual tribes and describes the expropriation and allottment of the land. Its focus is on the inheritance of Benjamin that lies between Judah and Joseph and includes Jerusalem (Josh 18). The surrounding chapters (Josh 16-17, 19-20) assign the cities of refuge and the territory of Simeon and the northern tribes. They are enclosed by the chapters that define the inheritances of Judah, Levi and the Transjordanian tribes (Josh 14-15, 21-22). The introductory and concluding chapters (Josh 12-13, 23-24) summarize the history and anticipate the problems that will be caused by Israel's assimilation to the nations that are left in the land.

The argument from analogy and polar opposition lets Dtr^2 preserve the Dtr^1 interpretation of a conquest by all Israel and simultaneously incorporate it into a more comprehensive theory. In the first part (Josh 1-8) Dtr^2 uses polar opposites to suppress the Dtr^1 conquest narrative and replace it with a theory of holy war. In the second part (Josh 9-11) Dtr^1's conquest of north and south is combined with variants that illustrate the theory of the ban, and with lists that limit the conquest to a few specific kings and cities. In the third part (Josh 12-24) Dtr^2 uses the argument from analogy to substitute the theory of tribal allottment for the Dtr^1 notion of a conquest by all the tribes of Israel.

F. The sixth book, Judges, is a Dtr^2 composition that describes the settlement of the individual tribes and reconstructs the antecedents of the monarchy (Fig 5: VI, A-E). Each of its parts has the usual topical arrangement, depends on the argument from analogy, and bases its interpretation on the balance of polar opposites.

1. The first part (Judges 1-5) is Dtr^2's summary of the conquest. It repeats information from the book of Joshua and explains that the tribes did not occupy all their allotted territory because the people abandoned the law and turned to other gods. The chapters are arranged symmetrically so that the failure of the individual tribes to conquer all their land

(Judg 1) matches the victory of allied tribes over Sisera (Judg 5), the conquest ascribed in general to Joshua is also attributed in particular to Deborah and Barak (Judg 2, 4), and the point of the whole story depends on the notion of divine testing (Judg 3). This arrangement gives prominence to the example of Othniel and the victory of Ehud, and distinguishes the two tribes, Benjamin and Judah, around which the action in the corresponding fifth part (Judg 17-21) revolves.

The polarity that this arrangement establishes between tribal initiative and national ideal is emphasized by the stark contrast between theory and narrative. Dtr^2's theory of repeated apostasy by all the people does not fit the stories of local harrassment, individual tribal response, and personal heroism to which it is affixed. But it expresses periodically and by polar opposition the point that Dtr^2 wants to make: the period of the settlement was the obverse of the era of the monarchy, the fragmentation of the tribes anticipated the formation of a national state, the people did what was evil in the sight of Yahweh or what was right in their own eyes because there was no king in Israel (Judg 17:6; 18:1; 19:1; 21:25).

2. The second part (Judg 6-9) compares the call of Gideon to the pretensions of Abimelek (Judg 6, 9) and contrasts Israel's victory over Midian with the conflict between Ephraim and Manasseh (Judg 7-8). Similarly, Abimelek is the polar opposite of Jerubbaal (Judg 6-8, 9) and together they represent Dtr^2's ambivalence toward kingship. Further, in the organization of the whole book, the story of Gideon is paired with the saga of Samson and together they illustrate the balance that Dtr^2 maintains between monarchical government and prophetic inspiration.[80]

3. The third part (Judg 10-12) has the same concentric arrangement. It focuses on Israel's victories in Transjordan (Judg 11:12-28) and compares them with the story of Jephthah's defeat of the Ammonites in Gilead (Judg 11:1-11, 29-40). It encloses these between contrasting interpretations of the Ammonite threat (Judg 10:6-16; 12:1-6), and includes the whole story in a time of prosperity marked by a continuous succession of judges (Judg 10:1-5; 12:7-14). This part has no polar

opposite but it records the repentance of the people (Judg 10:15-16) and the defeat of Ephraim (Judg 12:1-6) and is a turning point in the book.

4. The fourth part encloses Samson's outrageous treatment of the Philistines (Judg 14-15) in the story of his nazirite dedication (Judg 13, 16). He resembles Gideon in being called by God and then defecting, Samuel in his nazirite vocation and defeat of the Philistines, and Saul in his presumption and death.

5. The fifth part (Judg 17-21) matches the first by describing how the separate tribes achieved cohesion as the people of God in concerted action against the tribe of Benjamin. It also anticipates the early history of the monarchy by introducing all the groups, places and topics that are presumed known in the story of Samuel, Saul and David. The first and last chapters (Judg 17, 21) introduce Bethlehem and Jabesh Gilead that made and unmade Saul, and combine to insinuate that the Levitical priesthood was installed in the house of God at Shiloh. The second and fourth chapters (Judg 18, 20) introduce the shrines at Bethel and Dan and refer to the fall of the northern kingdom (Judg 18:30). The middle chapter (Judg 19) refers to Bethlehem and Jerusalem, the antithesis of Saul's kingdom, mentions Ramah, the home of Saul's nemesis Samuel, and compares Saul's hometown Gibeah to Sodom and Gomorrah.

The linear and periodic organization of the book lets Dtr[2] construct an era of tribal disintegration that anticipates the formation of the kingdom and reflects the condition of its destruction. There is the usual arrangement in which each part is related to the next, balanced by another, and interpreted by its opposite. But, in addition, the framework functions as a counterpoint to the stories, and each story is matched by a different one. In the first part, three chapters are concerned with the settlement of individual tribes (Judg 1-3), and two relate wars of conquest by the nation (Judg 4-5). In the second part, three chapters are devoted to Gideon (Judg 6-8) and one to Abimelek (Judg 9). In the third, there is the story of Jephthah and a separate history of the judges. In the fourth, the story of Samson ends after three chapters (Judg 13-15) and then continues in a fourth (Judg 16). In the fifth part, the migration of Dan (Judg 17-18) is juxtaposed to the diminution of Benjamin (Judg 19-21). History is not univocal and in Dtr^{2}'s estimation there is another side to everything.

G. The seventh book, I-II Samuel, describes the process that led to the unification of the tribes and the completion of the conquest under David (Fig 5: VII, A-F).[81] The first part (I Sam 1-7) contains Dtr^{1}'s story of the birth of Samuel but expands it into a history of the Philistine wars. The second part (I Sam 8-15) contains Dtr^{1}'s narrative of Saul's reign but changes it into a disquisition on the origins and limitations of kingship. The third part (I Sam 16 - II Sam 2) contains Dtr^{1}'s narrative of Saul's wars but develops it into a story of sedition and conspiracy on behalf of David. In the fourth part (II Sam 3-12) Nathan's oracle and Dtr^{1}'s narrative of the birth of Solomon are incorporated into a theory of history and divine government that attributes to David the culmination of the wilderness wanderings, the finalization of the conquest, the unification of the tribes, and the inauguration of a perpetual order. The fifth part (II Sam 13-19) contains the Dtr^{1} version of Absalom's revolt but changes it into a war between the kingdoms in which David won the allegiance of the north. The sixth part (II Sam 20-24) confirms the covenant with David and his victory over all the enemies of Israel.

The organization of the book emphasizes David's preeminence. The third and fourth parts describe the political and theological foundations of the Davidic dynasty, weighing charges of violence and conspiracy against the evidence of the dynastic promise and repeated covenants with the North. The second and fifth parts contrast the reign of Saul and the revolt of Absalom,[82] illustrating both the dynastic principle and divine repudiation of a separate northern kingdom. The first and sixth parts compare the eras of Samuel and David, their wars with the Philistines, their associations with Shiloh and Jerusalem, and their authority over all the tribes of Israel. This concentration on David lets Dtr^{2} balance the limitations of the monarchy against the theory of divine governance and weigh criticism of the kings against Yahweh'a choice of David and his successors.

H. The eighth book, I-II Kings, has seven parts and recounts the history of the nation from the accession of Solomon to the restoration of Jehoiakin (Fig 5: VIII, A-G). The first part (I Kgs 1-11) confirms the promise to David and describes the building of the temple. The last part (II Kgs 21-25) relates the destruction of the temple and the survival of the Davidic dynasty. The second part (I Kgs 12-15) records the rebellion of the north and the sin of Jeroboam and the sixth part (II Kgs 14-20) records the fall of the northern kingdom and the reform of Hezekiah. The third and the fifth parts (I Kgs 16-22; II Kgs 8-13) relate the crimes of Ahab in the north and the repercussions for Judah in the time of Athaliah. The central part (II Kgs 1-7) has no parallel but describes the power of the prophetic word that is supposed in all the other parts.

II. Style

The characteristic feature of Dtr^2's style is repetition.[83] It is the corollary of the linear logic, periodicity, and analogy that Dtr^2 used to organize diverse and difficult materials. It is specifically a function of commentary and interpretation and is used both to harmonize the sources and to make connections between the various parts of the history.

The three basic types of repetition are collected in the first wife-sister story (Gen 12:10-20).[84] First, Dtr^2 sets it apart as a parenthesis by repeating after its insertion the information that preceded it (Gen 13:1, 3-4 = 12:7, 8b-9 = Dtr^2). Secondly, Dtr^2 anticipates the alternate versions of the same story (Gen 20, 26) and constructs the incident entirely from their language.[85] Thirdly, Dtr^2 modifies the alternate versions by composing cross-references to its own story: the J version is modified by explicit reference to the example of Abraham (Gen 26:1a^b, 2-5); the E version is changed to include the healing of Abimelek (Gen 20:17-18) although it was Pharaoh who had been afflicted (Gen 12:17) and not Abimelek.

A. The first type of repetition is peculiar to Dtr^2's commentary on sources. For instance, Dtr^2 added a geography of the garden of Eden (Gen 2:10-14) and then repeated what J had narrated before the insertion (Gen 2:15 = 2:8). Similarly, Dtr^2

revised the covenant with Noah by including stipulations concerning blood (Gen 9:2-6), and then repeated P's introductory discourse (Gen 9:7-8 = 9:1). Again, after the insertion of the genealogy of Moses and Aaron (Exod 6:14-25), Dtr^2 repeats in inverse order what had preceded it (Exod 6:26-30 = 6:10-13). Or, the song of Moses is set apart by reduplicating its introit and the theme from P that it illustrates (Exod 15:19-21 = 14: 29 + 15:1). Or, again, the plans for the furnishings of the tent of meeting (Exod 25:9a^b, 10-39) end by repeating P's reference to the design revealed on the mountain (Exod 25:40 = 25:9a^{a}b). Or, further, the list of tribal leaders sent to reconnoiter the land (Num 13:4-15) concludes by repeating elements from its introduction (Num 13:16 = 13:2, 3, 4a). Similarly, Dtr^2's preface to Deuteronomy ends with an elaborate repetition of the Dtr^1 introduction that it displaced (Deut 4: 44-49 = 1:1a). Or, again, Dtr^2 changes Moses' farewell to the people (Deut 31:1-2a, 3a, 6) into the commissioning of Joshua (Deut 31:3b-4) but at the end of the insertion repeats what Dtr^1 had said in the beginning (Deut 31:5 = 31:3a). Similarly, Dtr^2 has the Jericho spies hang from the window and exonerate themselves with a legal fiction (Josh 2:17-20) but then it returns to Rahab's earlier suggestion that they go away (Josh 2: 21 = 2:16). Or, further, the battle between David and the Philistine is interrupted by an exposition of the principles of holy war (I Sam 17:42-47) but then Dtr^2 returns to the attack (I Sam 17:48 = 17:41). Similarly, in the affair of Uriah the Hittite, Dtr^2 interrupts the marriage of David and Bathsheba and the birth of Solomon (II Sam 11:27a^a + 12:24b^a) with the account of an illegitimate son who died (II Sam 11:27a^b-12:23) but eventually returns to the original story (II Sam 12:24a = 11:27a). Or, Dtr^2 adds the assertion that the golden calves were the sin of Jeroboam (I Kgs 12:30a) and then repeats that one was at Dan (I Kgs 12:30b = 12:29b). Similarly, Dtr^2 defends the revolt of Jehu by inserting a story about Elisha and the condemnation of the house of Ahab (II Kgs 9:1-13), but then repeats the introduction to the Dtr^1 narrative (II Kgs 9:14b-15 = 8:28-29).

A simpler and less obtrusive variant of this type of repetition consists in inserting a segment that begins like the passage it displaces. For instance, Hezekiah's tribute to

Sennacherib (II Kgs 18:14-16) begins like the Dtr^{1} narrative of Sennacherib's challenge that it displaces (*wayyišlaḥ*, II Kgs 18:14 = 18:17). The second embassy to Hezekiah that Dtr^{2} inserts (II Kgs 19:9b-36a^{a}) begins, like the Dtr^{1} sentence it displaces, with the return of Sennacherib (*wayyāšāb*, II Kgs 19: 9b = 19:36a^{b}b). Dtr^{2} adds a condemnation of Ahaziah (II Kgs 8: 27) that repeats the first word of the Dtr^{1} narrative that it preempts (*wayyēlek*, II Kgs 8:27 = 8:28). Solomon's execution of David's enemies (I Kgs 2:13-46a) was inserted into the Dtr^{1} narrative of the death of David and the accession of Solomon (I Kgs 2:10-11, 46b) and begins with Dtr^{2}'s version of the Dtr^{1} statement it displaces (I Kgs 2:12 = 2:46b). In the story of the garden of Eden Dtr^{2} added a series of curses (Gen 3:14-21) that begins like the J text it preempted (*wayyōʾmer yhwh ʾĕlōhîm*, Gen 3:14 = 3:22). Dtr^{2} also added the curse of Canaan (Gen 9: 20-27) but introduced it by combining the beginning and end of the P genealogy that it preempts (Gen 9:18-19 = 10:1, 31-32).

B. The second type of repetition contributes to the harmonization of the sources by establishing in advance the principles of their interpretation. It includes summaries, paradigms, and preemptive variants that are artificially constructed from the texts that they introduce and explain.

1. Summaries. The blessing of Abraham (Gen 12:2-3) combines elements from J, P, and E,[86] to introduce the Abraham cycle and preempt the other interpretations. Similarly, the first inclusive promise to Abraham (Gen 13:14-17) is a crasis of allusions to the Balaam oracles, the covenant with Abraham, and the vision of the land accorded to Moses,[87] and predicts the history of the nation up to the entry into the land. Further, Dtr^{2}'s covenant with Abraham (Gen 15) is a proleptic variant of the P version (Gen 17) that combines allusions to Dtr^{1}, P and E, and anticipates the history up to the occupation of the land.[88] Again, Dtr^{2}'s revision of the Joseph story includes a speech by Judah (Gen 44:18-34) that summarizes the whole story and also anticipates the distinction that Dtr^{2} makes between the house of Judah and the house of Joseph.[89] Similarly, the blessing of Jacob (Gen 49:1-28) recapitulates texts from other narratives and determines that the following history of Israel will be understood as the history of a tribal federation.[90] Also, Dtr^{2}'s anecdote about the Hebrew

midwives in Egypt (Exod 1:15-21) is an elaboration of two statements in the J narrative (Exod 1:16 = 1:22; 1:20b = 1:9) but it begins the humiliation of Pharaoh and the exaltation of Israel that Dtr^2 pursues in the story of the plagues.[91] Futher, the song of Moses (Exod 15:1-21) duplicates the exodus narratives (Exod 14) but it is also Dtr^2's paradigm of the conquest and settlement.[92] Or, similarly, Dtr^2 introduces the Sinai covenant with a preemptive interpretation (Exod 19:3b-6) that includes a summary of the exodus and a program for the future.[93] Or, again, Dtr^2 preempts the story of the spies (Num 13-14) by attributing the conquest to the tutelage of the ark (Num 10: 33-36) and describing its progress in the language of known texts.[94]

2. Paradigms. This type of repetition distinguishes Dtr^2's speeches and transitional syntheses,[95] and marks distinct phases in the argument or critical junctures in the interpretation.

The wilderness period, for instance, is introduced by two rebellions that Dtr^2 considers typical (Num 11; cf. Deut 9:22). The second rebellion is extremely complex. It combines a variant of the P story of the manna (Num 11:4-9, 18-23, 31-35; cp. Exod 16:1-3, 6-7, 9-15) with a variant of E's legislative reforms (Num 11:10-17, 24-30) and discusses the issues of leadership and authority that occupy this part of the history. The first rebellion is its paradigm and simplifies it by illustrating the pattern of rebellion and suggesting in advance the resolution of the issues (Num 11:1-3): the pattern is that at every stage of the journey (11:3) the people do wrong (11:1a), anger Yahweh (11:1b) and are punished (11:1b); the resolution of the issues is anticipated by the intercession of Moses when the people cry out for help (11:3).[96]

Similarly, the period of the judges is transitional to the final settlement of the land under David. It involves a complicated theory (Judg 2:1-3:6) that is illustrated in a series of individual histories and isolated incidents. But Dtr^2 simplifies the argument by making Othniel the paradigm of the histories (Judg 3:7-11) and by composing pointed interpretations of the isolated incidents.[97]

Similarly, Dtr^{2} considers that the events in Transjordan are a model for the conquest of the promised land.[98] The events at Baal Peor (Num 25:1-5), consequently, are typical of the problems involved in the conquest (Num 25:1-2 = Exod 34: 15-16) and are marked explicitly as a model of the era of the judges (Num 25:5; cp. Judg 2:1-5; 3:6).[99]

3. Variants. The preemptive variant anticipates and corrects the sources. For example, Dtr^{1} began the narrative of the conquest with an exhortation by Joshua that reaffirmed the Sinai covenant before the people crossed at Jericho (Josh 3:5, 10b, 16b, = Exod 34:10, 11b).[100] Dtr^{2} corrected this view of the conquest by distributing Joshua's exhortation in three distinct speeches (Josh 3:1-5, 6-8, 9-13) and then composing five consecutive interpretations of the crossing (Josh 3:14-17; 4:1-9, 10-13, 14-19, 20-24). Similarly, the law of centralization according to Dtr^{1} prescribed that holocausts should be offered at the sanctuary but allowed meat to be eaten anywhere (Deut 12:13-14, 20, 26). But Dtr^{2} considers that eating meat is a sacrifice and that sacrifice should be offered at the central sanctuary, and includes the Dtr^{1} law in a system of iteration that preempts and revises it. The first iteration (Deut 12:1-7) centralizes sacrifice as a precaution against false worship; the second iteration (Deut 12:8-12) makes the centralization of sacrifice a corollary of the conquest; the third (Deut 12:13-19) allows some sacrifice away from the central sanctuary but surrounds it with prescriptions and obligations; the fourth iteration (Deut 12:20-27) emphasizes that this is an exception and insists that the sacrificial rituals be followed even away from the sanctuary; the fifth iteration (Deut 12:28-31) returns to the warning against false worship and abominable sacrifice. Gradually, in this process of iteration, the Dtr^{1} legislation is completely lost and assimilated to the Dtr^{2} interpretation.

A comparable system of iteration is used to adapt the Dtr^{1} version of Nathan's oracle to Dtr^{2}'s perspective. The original oracle is a word of Yahweh promising David dynastic succession (II Sam 7:4b-5a, 12, 14a, 15a, 16a, 17a^{a}b). Dtr^{2} applied the promise to the relationship between Yahweh and Israel, and specifically to the construction of the temple, by incorporating the oracle into a whole series of speeches. A preface (II Sam 7:1-3) relativizes the dynasty by giving the word *bêt* an alternate and conflicting meaning. A preemptive vision reviews the history of Israel from Egypt through the period of the judges to the time of David and transfers the promise to the people (II Sam 7:4-11a). The oracle itself is changed (II Sam 7:11b-17) to emphasize the defection of past and future kings, to include the building of the temple, and to promise David enduring authority (*kissēʾ*) rather than perpetual dominion (*mamlākâ*). Finally, the revised and expanded oracle is joined to a complementary version in which David affirms his faith in the prophetic word and in the enduring relationship between Yahweh and Israel (II Sam 7:18-29). In the process of iteration the idea of a dynasty gradually fades and is subsumed in Yahweh's fidelity to the people.

Similarly, the P sanctuary is gradually converted into the Dtr^{2} tent of meeting by adding instructions on its furnishings and dimensions (Exod 25:6-7, 9a^{b}, 10-40; 26:31-37; 27:1-21). Or, the J Sinai convenant (Exod 34) is changed from a promise of conquest into a promise of divine guidance by adding a series of prior manifestations and discussions that preempt it (Exod 33:1-23; 34:8-9). Or, the rebellion led by Dathan and Abiram is changed into a dispute concerning religious jurisdiction by adding the story of Korah (Num 16:1-11, 15-24, 25b-27a, 32b, 33b, 35). Or, the revolt of Adonijah and the coronation of Solomon is turned into a story of palace intrigue by adding a preface portraying David's senility (I Kgs 1:1-4). Or, the anointing of David by all the tribes of Israel (II Sam 5:1a, 3b) is changed into the confirmation of his kingship over the North by inserting a speech (5:1b-2), a duplicate embassy (5:3a), and a regnal formula (5:4-5). Or, the Dtr^{1} version of Saul's coronation (Fig 2: IV, 1-8) is preempted by two contrary versions (I Sam 9-11) and two diatribes (I Sam 8, 12) inserted by Dtr^{2}. Or, Dtr^{1}'s covenant at Horeb (Fig 2: I, 1-3) is anticipated and replaced by the Dtr^{2} version (Deut 4). Or, Dtr^{1}'s explanation of the fall of Samaria (Fig 2: VIII, 27) is preempted by Dtr^{2}'s interpretation (II Kgs 17).

C. The third type of repetition is cross-reference. It is used either to harmonize the sources and homogenize the text, or to relate separate issues and interpretations by prolepsis and resumption, or to combine and juxtapose materials by a process of inclusion.

1. Harmonization. Simple cross-referencing assimilates the sources to their interpretations. For instance, J's fashioning of Adam (Gen 2:7a) is related to P's idea of creation by inserting the designation "living creature" (Gen 2:7b [Dtr^2]; cp. Gen 1:20). Or, the story of Noah is referred back to the story of the garden of Eden by repeating that the land was cursed (Gen 5:29b^b). Or, Dtr^2 justifies the inclusion of seven pairs of clean and unclean animals (Gen 7:2-3, 8) by repeating P's stipulation concerning pairs of animals (Gen 7:9; cp. Gen 6:19). Or, Dtr^2 explains the separation of Abraham and Lot by repeating J's reason (Gen 13:2, 5) in the language of P (Gen 13:6; cp. Gen 12:5). Or, the fact that Isaac and Rebeccah had favorites (Gen 25:28) connects P's story that Esau sold his birthright (Gen 25:29-34) with the J narrative that Jacob stole his blessing (Gen 27). Or, the J story of Abraham and the three men is introduced as an apparition of Yahweh (Gen 18:1a) to make it resemble P's covenant with Abraham (Gen 17). Or, Isaac is moved from Gerar to Beersheba simply by referring to the wells his father had dug (Gen 26:15, 18). Or, P's list of the sons of Israel is assimilated to Dtr^2's genealogy by recalling that there were seventy descendants of Jacob in Egypt (Exod 1:5a = Gen 46:27). Or, in the spy story, P's description of the inhabitants of the land (Num 13:32, 33b) is referred back to J's (Num 13:22a) by identifying them as Nephilim (Num 13:33a). Or, the story of Saul is filled with cross-references to the covenant with David.[101]

2. Prolepsis and Resumption. The most common form of repetition and the simplest way of reinterpreting the sources is prolepsis and resumption.[102] For instance, in the flood story Dtr^2 distinguishes between clean and unclean animals (Gen 6:7a^b; 7:2-3, 8, 23a*) in preparation for the sacrifice that Noah offers (Gen 8:20-22). Similarly, the remark that Sarah was barren (Gen 11:30) is proleptic to the covenant with

Abraham (Gen 15) and its variants. Or, since the story of Abraham and Lot is interrupted by other incidents (Gen 14-17), Dtr^2 includes proleptic references to the destruction of Sodom and Gomorrah (Gen 13:10b, 13). Similarly, Yahweh's soliloquy before the destruction of Sodom and Gomorrah resumes the blessings and promises to Abraham (Gen 18:17-19 = 12:2-3; 15: 1-6). Or, Rebecca's dislike of Hittite women (Gen 27:46) is a resumptive reference to Esau's wives (Gen 26:34-35). Or, the mention of store-cities that the Israelites built in Egypt (Exod 1:11b) is proleptic to the dispute between Moses and the foremen (Exod 5:1-6:1). Or, the despoiling of the Egyptians (Exod 3:21-22) and the death of the Egyptian first-born (Exod 4:21-23) anticipate the conclusion of the plague story (Exod 11:1-8; 12:29-36). Or, the consecration of mount Sinai (Exod 19:12-13, 21-25) is proleptic to the concluding covenant (Exod 24:1-11). Or, war is declared against the Midianites (Num 25:16-18) and then takes place (Num 31). Or, the defeat of Sihon and Og (Deut 1:4) is proleptic to Dtr^2's retelling of the story (Deut 2:26-3:11). Or, the death of Moses and the succession of Joshua are announced at the beginning of the book (Deut 1:37-38) and resumed at the end (Deut 31, 34). Or, Moses orders the people to set up inscribed stones when they cross the Jordan and enter the land (Deut 27: 1-8) and both commands eventually are obeyed (Josh 3-4; 8:30-35). Or, Joshua's curse on Jericho (Josh 6:26) falls in the time of Ahab (I Kgs 16:34). Or, the covenant on Horeb proleptically includes the Gibeonites who would otherwise have been an occasion of its violation (Deut 29:10; Josh 9:27). Or, the covenant with David includes a proleptic reference to the temple (II Sam 7:13) that is resumed in Solomon's prayer at its dedication (I Kgs 8:18-20). Or, Jeroboam is included proleptically in the Shechem convention (I Kgs 12:2-3a, 12) to anticipate his coronation (I Kgs 12:20a) and to make him responsible for the schism as Ahijah had predicted (I Kgs 11: 27-39).

3. Inclusion. The compositional equivalent of repetition by cross-referencing is inclusion. It is a feature of texts composed by Dtr^2 and consists in interrupting a story that has begun or a topic that has been introduced with

extraneous but analogous material.

For instance, Dtr^1 concludes the covenant at Horeb with the impending death of Moses and the assurance of the conquest (Deut 31:1-2a, 3a, 6), but Dtr^2 adds the succession of Joshua, the model conquest of Sihon and Og, and an oblique reference to the law of the ban (Deut 31:2b, 3b-5). Then Dtr^2 repeats some of the same material to commission Joshua (Deut 31:7-8), but inserts instructions for the reading of the law (31:9-13), then returns to the commissioning of Joshua (31:14-15) but interrupts with an introduction to the song of Moses (31:16-22), then returns to the commissioning of Joshua (31:23), mentions the book of the law again (31:24-26) and finally returns to the song of Moses (31:27-29). The arrangement establishes a relationship between diverse and contrary elements that are crucial to Dtr^2's interpretation: in the end both the law and the song witness against the people (Deut 31:26, 28; 32:44-47); subsequently, Joshua and the book of the law are associated in the conquest (Josh 1:6-9; 8:30-35).

A similar literary construction is used in the composition of Dtr^2's paradigmatic rebellions in the wilderness (Num 11). The story of Taberah (Num 11:1-3) is the model for the rebellion at Kibrot Hattaawah (11:4-35) and includes the complaint of the people, the anger of Yahweh, the intercession of Moses, and the name of the place. The story of Kibrot Hattaawah begins with the complaint (11:4-6) but interrupts the pattern with a parenthesis on the manna (11:7-9), then continues with the anger of Yahweh (11:10) but interrupts the pattern with Moses' unwillingness to intercede and Yahweh's reply (11:11-17), then returns to the rebellion with a threat of punishment (11:18-23) but interrupts again with the continuation of Yahweh's reply to Moses (11:24-25), adds a digression on prophecy (11:26-30), and finally returns to the pattern with the anger of Yahweh and the name of the place (11:31-35). The digression on prophecy is proleptic to the following story of Miriam and Aaron (Num 12) but the other intertwined stories let Dtr^2 develop a theory of authority and divine guidance that is used later to interpret, for instance, the conquest (Deut 1:9-18, 30-33) or life in the wilderness (Deut 8:2-6).

The same technique is used to combine the law and the covenant at Sinai (Exod 24). Moses and Aaron, Aaron's sons, and the elders of Israel are summoned to the mountain and are told to worship at a distance (Exod 24:1). But this topic is dropped and Moses is told to approach Yahweh (Exod 24:2). And then instead of approaching Yahweh Moses goes to the people, reads the law, and makes a covenant (Exod 24:3-8). But then Moses, Aaron and his sons, and the elders go to the mountain and see God (24:9-11). And, finally, Moses approaches Yahweh (24:12-18). This inclusion resumes the instructions given earlier (Exod 19:12-25), anticipates the selection of seventy elders as prophets (Num 11), incorporates the P and E versions of revelation at Sinai (Exod 24:13-18), and preempts J's version of the covenant (Exod 34).

Similarly, the Dtr^2 covenant with Abraham opens with the question of descendants (Gen 15:1-6), breaks off to begin a covenant ritual (15:7-11), returns to Abraham's descendants (15:12-16) and ends by concluding the covenant (15:17-21). Or, Abraham's negotiations with the king of Sodom (Gen 14:17, 21-24) are interrupted by the blessing of Melchizedek (Gen 14:18-20). Or, Dtr^2 interrupts its own version of Passover (Exod 12:7, 12-13, 21-27) with the ritual for the feast of Unleavened Bread that replaces it (Exod 12:14-20). Or, Dtr^2's review of events from Egypt to Transjordan begins with the journey from Horeb to Qadesh Barnea (Deut 1:1-4), returns to Horeb (1:5-8) but interrupts the story to appoint leaders (1:9-18), returns to the journey from Horeb to Qadesh Barnea (1:19-21), introduces the spy narrative (1:22-29), returns to the question of leadership (1:30-33), continues the spy narrative (1:34-36), returns to the matter of leadership (1:37-38), comes back to the journey (1:39-40) and finishes with the conclusion of the spy narrative (1:41-46). Or, the story of the house of Eli moves from the crimes of his sons (I Sam 2:12-17) to the story of Samuel and his family (2:18-21), back to Eli's rebuke of his sons (2:22-25), then to the story of Samuel (2:26) and back to the house of Eli (2:27-36), then to Samuel's prophetic calling (3:1-14) and back to the house of Eli (3:15-18), then to Samuel (3:19-21), and finally to Eli and his sons (4:1-22). Or, the story of Josiah's reform (II Kgs 22:3-20; 23:4-20, 24-

25) is interrupted by readings from the book of the covenant (II Kgs 23:1-3, 21-23).

Repetition gives the history coherence despite the diverse materials and incongruous viewpoints that it contains. It contributes to the organic arrangement of the history, harmonizes the versions and interpretations, and dissipates the differences among the sources. It is the most distinctive feature of Dtr^2's style and it makes the history almost indistinguishable from its antecedents.

III. Language

The characteristic language of Dtr^2 is both eclectic and specific. In commenting on the sources Dtr^2 imitates them and uses their language. But in incorporating the sources into a general system of interpretation Dtr^2 also uses specific, technical and conceptual language.[103] The eclectic quality of the language assimilates Dtr^2 to the sources. The attempt to be specific entails redundancy, reduplication, and patterns of recurrence that distinguish Dtr^2 from the sources. Both of these characteristics can be illustrated by considering the relationship between the individual sources and the Dtr^2 interpretation.

A. Dtr^2's commentary of E follows a regular pattern. First, it repeats part of the E text, verbatim or with slight variation. Then it inserts the name Yahweh, and may insert elements from an apposite J text. Finally it adds specific Dtr^2 ideas and interests in language that is pedantic, predictable, or redundant. For example:

Dtr^2 interprets (Exod 3:15) E's revelation of God's name to Moses at the mountain (Exod 3:9-14) by repeating the E text (3:15a = 3:6a, 13, 14), inserting the name Yahweh (3:15a; cp. 3:13), and adding a repetitive statement to comment on the name (3:15b "This is my name for ever, and this is my memorial from generation to generation").

In the E version, Jethro came to meet Moses at the mountain of God, brought him his wife and children, and suggested a reform of the judicial system (Exod 18:1a, 2a, 3-5, 12-27). The Dtr^2 version begins by repeating the E text (18:6 [= 18:5]: "I am your father-in-law Jethro, coming to you with your wife and her two sons"), inserts the name Yahweh and retells the exodus (18:7-8), and finally develops a typical argument on the supremacy of Yahweh that repeats three times Israel's deliverance from the hands of the Egyptians (18:8-11; cp. Deut 4:32-40; 7:6-11).

Dtr[2] revised E's story of the sacrifice of Isaac by adding duplicate speeches by an angel (Gen 22:11-12, 14, 15-18). The name Yahweh was inserted into the identification of the angel, the mountian, and the promise (22:11, 14-16). The E text was repeated in the command not to touch the boy (22:12 = 22:10), and in the recognition that Abraham had not withheld his only son (22:12 = 22:2). The idea that the angel called out from heaven (22:11, 15) is taken verbatim from E's story of Hagar and Ishmael (Gen 21:17). The expression "He said 'Abraham, Abraham' and he said 'Here I am'" (22:11b) repeats E (22:1) and imitates E's style (Gen 46:2; Exod 3:4) and is not Dtr[2]'s proper language (cp. I Sam 3:4, 10). Finally, Dtr[2] adds its own typical ideas in redundant and repetitive cadences: the angel of Yahweh calls out twice from heaven (22:11, 15); the angel's command both repeats E (22:12 "Do not touch the boy" = 22:10) and adds Dtr[2]'s own version (22:12 "and do not do anything to him"); in naming the mountain Dtr[2] juxtaposes "Yahweh will see" and Yahweh will be seen" (22:14); three reasons are given for the promises (22:16b, 18b: "Since you did this, and did not withhold your son, your only son; since you obeyed me"): and the promises are applied in three different ways to Abraham's offspring (22:17-18a).

Dtr[2] revised E's version of the wife-sister story to make it clear that Abraham, and not Abimelek, was the father of Isaac (Gen 20:1a[b], 4-7, 9, 12-13, 17-18). Dtr[2] adds the name Yahweh (20:18) and the designation 'Lord' (20:4) that is reserved for Yahweh (e.g. Gen 18:3, 27, 31; 19:18), repeats the language of E (20:5-7 = 20:2-3), and alludes to the J version of the story (20:6-7, "touch, die" = Gen 26:11). Then Dtr[2] adds issues of recurrent interest for the history such as sin, prophetic intercession and divine healing, and expresses them in technical and redundant language: that Abimelek had not approached Sarah means that the marriage had not been consummated (20:4; Deut 22:14); Abimelek uses forensic language to plead his case, claiming innocence (20:4; Deut 25:1), integrity (20:5 *bĕtam lĕbābî* = I Kgs 9:4) and immunity (20:5 *beniqyôn kappay* = Num 5:31); Yahweh replies in kind, confirming Abimelek's integrity, insisting that there has not been a crime (20:6, *ngᶜ* = Deut 17:8) or a sin (20:6; Deut 19:15), but warning him that if he does not return Abraham's wife he will die (20:7; Deut 22:22); then Dtr^2 copies the E text by having Abimelek ask Abraham what he has done (20:9 = 20:10) but twice adds the technical term 'sin' (20:9a) and repeats the protest that Abraham has done deeds that ought not to be done (20:9b).

This pattern is applied without exception every time that Dtr^2 comments on E, and its intrusion explains some obvious anomalies in the text: the insertion of redundant laws (Exod 22:9-19); the adventitious resemblance between E's ritual calendar and J's (Exod 23:17-19; 34:23, 25-26); the changes to E's promise of divine guidance that make it resemble the text of J's Sinai covenant (Exod 23:23-25a, 31b-33; cp. 34:12-13, 15-16); the additions to the story of the golden calf that interpret it as idolatry and the sin of Jeroboam (Exod 32:5-6a, 7-14, 26-35; cp. I Kgs 12:28b, 30-33; 13:33-34); the intrusion of the decalogue (Exod 20:2-21:1); the transferal of the promises from Abraham to Jacob (Gen 28:13-16, 21b; 32:10-13); and the presence of God with Joseph in a foreign land (Gen 39:2-3, 5, 21-23).

B. Dtr^2 follows essentially the same plan in commenting on P. It repeats elements of the P text. It inserts topics of its own interest, sometimes with allusions to J or E. Then it elaborates on the topics with its peculiar and specific language. For instance.

In the story of Jacob and Esau P omits the theme of conflict that predominates in J and has Jacob travel to Paddan Aram to find a wife (Gen 28:1-5). Dtr^2 uses the occasion to complete the list of Esau's wives (Gen 28:6-9). The item begins by paraphrasing the P text (28:6 = 28:1-5), repeats that Jacob went to Paddan Aram (28:7b = 28:5), but combines the repetition with an allusion to the obedience of Jacob in J (28:7a = 27:43), repeats Isaac's disapproval of the Canaanite women (28:8 = 28:1), and ends with a name of Esau's wife that is a variant to P (28:9; cp. Gen 36:3). The text has two parts, the first repeating P's story of Jacob (28:6-7), the second modeled on the first and repeating all its basic ideas to tell the story of Esau (28:8-9).

Dtr^2 changes the covenant with Noah by inserting a brief ethical treatise (Gen 9:2-8). It uses P's list of creatures (9:2a^{b}b = 8:17; 9:10), refers to P's text on the creation of man (9:6b = 1:26-27), formulates a dietary law on the model of P's creation account (9:3 = 1:30) and concludes by repeating the P text to which it was attached (9:7-8 = 9:1). But its principal purpose is to forbid the eating and shedding of blood (9:4-6) and its prohibitions are filled with assonance and raw repetition, most notably at the beginning (9:4 *ɔak bāśār bĕnapšô damô loɔ toɔkēlû*) and the end (9:6a *šōpēk dam hāɔādām bāɔādām dāmô yiššāpēk*). These topics are of special interest to Dtr^2 and recur elsewhere in the history (e.g. Num 35:33-34; Deut 12:23-25). The dietary law, besides, is combined with the formulas that Dtr^2 uses later to assure Israel of the conquest (9:2a^a, "the fear and dread of you" + 9:2b "into your hand they are given" = Deut 2:24-25).

After the covenant with Noah Dtr^2 relates the curse of Canaan (Gen 9:18-27). It begins with a summary of P genealogical texts (9:18-19 = 8:18; 10:1, 32), inserts topics of interest to Dtr^2 such as blessing and curse and the incestuous habits of the nations (cp. Gen 19:30-38), and is filled with assonance and reduplication.

At the end of the Jacob story P mentioned that Israel was blessed in Egypt, noted Jacob's age, and recorded his death (Gen 47:27-28; 49:33b). E added Jacob's blessing of Ephraim and Manasseh (Gen 48:1-2, 8-21) and his burial in the land of Canaan (Gen 50:1-8, 14). Dtr^2 inserted Jacob's blessing on the twelve tribes (Gen 48:22-49:28) and wrote another version of his burial that corrects E and supplements P. This Dtr^2 composition (Gen 47:29-31; 48:3-7; 49:29-33a; 50:9-13) relies on E for its plot[104] but gets its language mainly from P. When Jacob summons Joseph to his sickbed the conversation follows the pattern of the oath that Abraham imposed on his servent (Gen 24:2-9 = Dtr^2) but also alludes to P's story of the purchase of Macphelah (Gen 47:30; Gen 23). Jacob's autobiographical summary (48:3-7) combines quotations from P's revelation at Bethel (48:3-4 = 35:9, 11-12) with a resume of E's story of the birth of Ephraim and Manasseh (48:5a = 41:50-52) and with cross-references to the birth of Reuben and Simeon (48:5b = 29:31-33) and the death of Rachel (48:7 = 35:16, 19). The resumption of Jacob's command is a pastiche of P texts (49:29-33a = 23; 25:9-10; 35:27-29) combined with Dtr^2's mention of Rachel and Leah for the sake of genealogical completeness (Gen 49:31a[b]b). Finally, Jacob's burial at Macphelah refers to the same complex of texts (50:13; cf. Gen 23) but it is linked artificially to the E text (50:9 *wayyaᶜal ᶜimmô* = 50:7b *wayya-ᶜălû ᵓittô*) and is combined with Dtr^2's interest in obedience and the meaning of geographical names (Gen 50:10-12).

Dtr^2 revised P's legislation concerning Passover by combining it with the story of the death of the first-born (Exod 12:7, 12-13, 21-27, 29-32) and by aligning it with the festival of Unleavened Bread (Exod 12:14-20). The connection with the death of the first-born is peculiar to Dtr^2 but is made to appear like a P idea by a proleptic insertion into the P text (Exod 12:7) and by a resumptive repetition of P's instructions (Exod 12:21 = 12:3). The alignment with Unleavened Bread is also original to Dtr^2 but it is accomplished by an astute redeployment of P texts. Dtr^2 begins by imitating the introduction to P's legislation, giving to the first day of the festival the aura that P ascribed to the first month (Exod 12:14a[a] = 12:2). Then Dtr^2 synchronizes the feast of Unleavened Bread with the date that P assigned to Passover (Exod 12:18a = 12:2, 6) and identifies it with P's festival of the exodus (Exod 12:17a = 12:41b). Finally, Dtr^2 confirms this new legislation by repeating all its terms at least twice: the festival of Unleavened Bread is a perpetual statute for all generations (Exod 12:14b, 17b); Unleavened Bread is to be eaten for seven days and whoever eats leaven will be cut off from Israel (Exod 12:15, 19-20); the first day and the seventh day are specified and then fixed on the calendar (Exod 12:16, 18).

This pattern is applied in all Dtr^2 commentaries on P: in the genealogies (Gen 10:8-19, 21, 24-30; 11:29-30; 25:1-6; 36:9-43; 46:8-27); in the plague narratives (Fig 5: II, B, 2-6); in the wilderness rebellions (e.g. Exod 14:11-14), the construction of the tent of meeting (Fig 5: II, E, G), and the account of the death of Moses (Num 20:26, 28a^{a}, 29b^{b}; Deut 34: 1a^{b}, 6, 10-12). The use and imitation of P tend to confound Dtr^{2} and the source, but reference to special interests that recur throughout the history and reliance on specific and repetitive language maintain their distinction.

C. Dtr^{2} adapts the same pattern in commenting on Dtr^{1}. It repeats a specific word or phrase from the Dtr^{1} text. It elaborates on the point it has isolated, usually with reference to one of the other sources or with cross-reference to itself. Then it repeats the point, illustrates it, or describes its polar opposite, in its own specific and redundant language. For example:

After the death of Saul, in the Dtr^{1} narrative, all the tribes came to Hebron and anointed David king of Israel (II Sam 5:1a, 3b). Dtr^{2} thinks that David was already king of Judah and that it was only the northern tribes that came to Hebron (II Sam 5:1b-3a, 4-5). The revision takes place by repeating Dtr^{1}'s statement "they came to Hebron" (5:3a = 5:1a), by adding that David was already king (5:3a), and by substituting "elders" for "tribes". Then Dtr^{2} elaborates on the statement by affirming that the elders made a treaty with David (5:3a^{b}) and by repeating their oath of loyalty that is taken from earlier texts in the history (5:1b-2; cf. Gen 2:23; I Sam 13:14; 16:11; 18:13 etc.). Then Dtr^{2} repeats the point by giving David's regnal formula that confirms that David was king of Judah in Hebron before he became king of Israel in Jerusalem (5:4-5).

In the story of the rape of Tamar Dtr^{1} narrates that she begged Amnon not to force her and that he refused to listen (II Sam 13:12a^{a}, 14a). Dtr^{2} repeats exactly the same thing (13:16) and then develops a legal interpretation of the case (13:16-18). Tamar appeals to the law which states that a man who seduces a virgin must marry her, or pay a fine if her father refuses her in marriage, and may not ever divorce her (13:2a^{b}, 12a^{b}b-13, 16-18; cf. Exod 22:15-16; Deut 22:28-29). The argument is technical but it acquires emotional force by alluding to the Joseph story and the example of violence done to an innocent child by its siblings (*kĕtonet passîm*, 13:18, 19a^{b}; Gen 37:3, 23, 32). But then Dtr^{2} repeats the point of this interpretation

(13:20-22), noting Absalom's hatred of Amnon for having forced his sister (13:22b = 13:12a^{a}), remarking on her father's anger (13:21), objecting that the laws cited by Tamar did not apply because Amnon was her brother (13:20a), and observing that Tamar, because she was no longer a virgin, could never be married (13:20b; Deut 22:13-21). In the Dtr^{1} narrative the rape of Tamar is Absalom's motive for killing Amnon. Dtr^{2} justifies the killing of Amnon by proving the injustice he had done, and then by appealing to the precedent of death in cases of public outrage (*nĕbalâ*, 13:12b; cf. Gen 34:7; Deut 22:21; Josh 7:15; Judg 20:6, 10).

According to Dtr^{1} the revolt of Absalom involved people from all the tribes of Israel who came to the king for judgement (II Sam 15:1-3, 7b, 9-10). Dtr^{2} repeats that all Israel came to the king for judgement (15:6a = 15:2b) but limits the revolt to the northern tribes (15:4-7a, 8, 11-12). It elaborates on Absalom's response to the suppliants by inserting a duplicate speech (15:4a^{a} = 15:3a^{a}) that contains references to Dtr^{2}'s judicial reforms (15:4a^{b}b = Deut 17:8-13; 25:1; I Kgs 8:32), and by explicitly confining the revolt to the men of the northern kingdom (15:5-6). But then Dtr^{2} repeats the point of this interpretation by limiting the conspiracy to a few in Jerusalem who were deceived (15:11-12) and by comparing the revolt to Absalom's personal vendetta against Amnon (15:7a, 8).

In the Dtr^{1} narrative the revolt of Adonijah begins when he acquires a retinue and invites all his brothers, except Solomon, to a feast (I Kgs 1:5, 9a^{a}b^{a}, 10). Dtr^{2} repeats and enlarges the list of conspirators (1:7-8), elaborates with cross-references to the revolt of Absalom (1:6, 9a^{b}) and implies that the revolt affected all of Judah (1:9b^{b}). But then Dtr^{2} repeats the point of this interpretation by describing the counter-intrigue that led to the coronation of Solomon (1:1-4, 11-31, 35-37, 39a^{a}).

Dtr^{1} attributes the northern schism to Rehoboam's inexperience and to his negotiation in bad faith (I Kgs 12:1, 3b-4, 6-11, 13-15a, 20a). Dtr^{2} inserts Jeroboam at the beginning of the negotiations by repeating information that Dtr^{1} includes in other contexts (12:2-3a = 11:40 + 12:20a). Then Dtr^{2} elaborates with cross-references to the oracle of Ahijah and attributes the schism to divine providence (12:5, 12, 15b-19). And then Dtr^2 repeats the point of this interpretation by adding another incident that confirms that the division of the kingdom was in accordance with the word of Yahweh (12:21-24).

Dtr^1 describes Jeroboam's political motives for making the golden calves and placing them at Bethel and Dan (I Kgs 12:26, 27a, 28a, 29). Dtr^2 repeats some of the Dtr^1 text (12: 27b, 30b), quotes from the parallel rebellion at mount Sinai (12:28b = Exod 32:4b) and interprets the calves as the sin of Jeroboam (12:30). But then Dtr^2 gives another evaluation of Jeroboam's actions (12:25, 31-33) that concentrates on Bethel and repeatedly condemns him for the same offenses.

Dtr^1 assigns the beginning of Assyrian domination to the reign of Ahaz and the circumstances of the Syro-Ephraimite war (II Kgs 16:2a, 5, 7-9a, 20). Dtr^2 repeats the Dtr^1 text on the accession of Ahaz (16:1b = 15:38b), and then elaborates by adding the usual synchronism and evaluation (16:1a, 2b-4), and by inserting a cross-reference to the history of Elath (16:6; cf. 14:22). Finally, Dtr^2 repeats the point of this elaboration by giving another perspective on Assyrian domination that emphasizes the ritual aspects of Ahaz's apostasy (16:10-19).

Dtr^1 narrates that Amaziah was the son of Jehoaddin and reigned in Jerusalem, that he executed his father's assassins but was also the victim of a conspiracy, that he was buried with his fathers in the city of David and was succeeded by his own son (II Kgs 14:2, 5, 19-21). Dtr^2 repeats the accession of Amaziah (14:1b = 12:22b) and adds a synchronism with Jehoahaz of Israel (14:1a). Then it elaborates with an evaluation that refers back to his father's reign (14:3-4 = 12:3-4) and with a cross-reference to legislation limiting the death penalty (14:6 = Deut 24:16). Finally it relates the conspiracy to conflict with the northern kingdom by describing a battle in which Judah was defeated by Israel, Jerusalem was attacked, and the treasuries were despoiled (14:7-16).

Dtr^2 uses this pattern to incorporate and correct Dtr^1. It uses little of the Dtr^1 text, converts it into its own specific language, preempts its interpretation by adding another, and incorporates it into a complex system of iteration.

The result is a unified text in which Dtr[1] can be distinguished only as the single and unrepeated text.

D. Dtr[2]'s interpretation of J follows a similar but simpler pattern. It repeats part of the J text. It inserts its own topics and interests, sometimes with allusion to P, or to E with the insertion of the divine name Elohim. Finally, it relies on technical language or repetition to make its point. For instance:

J narrates that God made birds and animals as possible companions for man (Gen 2:18-19a[a], 20b). Dtr[2] brings them to man to be named (2:19a[b]b-20a) as a sign of man's dominion over them (cf. Gen 1:26, P). To do this Dtr[2] uses J's idea that God brought the woman to the man (2:19a[b] = 2:22b) and repeats J's mention of birds and animals (2:20a = 2:19a[a]). But Dtr[2] also adds redundant designations for the animals taken from P (2:19b, *nepeš ḥayyâ* = 1:20, 24, 28, 30; 2:20a[a], *bĕhēmâ* = 1: 24, 25, 26) and repeats three times that man gave them names.

J narrates that the sons of God married women and that their offspring were the famous heros of the past (Gen 6:1-2, 4a[b]b). Dtr[2] corrects J's anthropology and rewrites the story with genealogical information (6:3-4a[a]). The correction begins by quoting the beginning of Yahweh's soliloquy in J (6:3a = 6:7a) and ends by repeating the J text that preceded it (6:4a[a] = 6:2). The genealogical notice uses the contrast between flesh and spirit that P had proposed (6:3a = 6:17; 7:15) and identifies the heros with the more mundane Nephilim (6:4; cp. Num 13:33). This Dtr[2] revision also uses technical language (6:3 *lōᵓ yādôn*) and repetitive balance ("not forever" // "for 120 years", 6:3).

J narrates that Yahweh told Abraham to leave home and travel to the land he would show him (Gen 12:1). Dtr[2] changed the journey into a paradigm of Israel's relationship to the nations (Gen 12:2-3) by quoting a blessing that J reserves for Jacob (12:3a = Gen 27:29b; Num 24:9b), by referring to a promise in P's covenant with Abraham (12:2a[a] = Gen 17:5-6, 20), and by alluding to P's idea of the family of nations (12:3b[b] = Gen 10:5, 20, 31). Dtr[2]'s peculiar contribution to the passage consists in balancing "great nation" and "great name" (12:2a) and in repeating different aspects of the verb "bless" (12:2-3).

J narrates that Lot and his family did not escape the destruction of Sodom and Gomorrah (Gen 19:12-13a, 14, 24a, 25, 27a, 28). But Dtr^2 thinks that they did because Abraham interceded for them (Gen 18:22-33; 19:13b, 15-23, 24b, 26, 27b) and adds a summary statement to confirm this interpretation (Gen 19:29). This statement repeats key words and expressions the J used (cf. Gen 19:13a, 25) but is filled with pedantic repetition: "the overthrow when God overthrew" (19:29b); "when he destroyed the cities of the valley" (19:29a[a]) and "when he overthrew the cities" (19:29b[b]); "he sent Lot ... where Lot lived" (19:29b).

J narrates that Joseph's brothers returned to Egypt with Benjamin and were invited to dine with him (Gen 43:1-11, 13, 14b, 15a[a]b-17, 23b, 24b-29a, 30-32a, 33). Dtr^2 uses the occasion to review the story and comment on the providence of God (43:12, 14a, 15a[b], 18-23a, 24a, 29b, 32b, 34). It repeats at the beginning and the end J's statement that they were brought to Joseph's house (43:18a, 24a = 43:17b). It repeats the story, has the brothers identify the problem and then explain it to the steward (43:18a[a], 20b-21a), insists on the key words and expressions (43:18, 21-23), and is filled with assonance and repetitive cadences (43:18b, 19-20a).

J narrates that when Israel became too strong in Egypt Pharaoh ordered the death of their male children (Exod 1:8-11a, 12a, 22). Dtr^2 includes these points (Exod 1:16b, 20b) in a story that emphasizes the distinctiveness of Israel (Exod 1:15-21). This story uses the name God (1:17, 20, 21) and repeats twice that the midwives feared God (1:17, 21), that they were not needed (1:16, 19) and that they disobeyed the king of Egypt (1:17, 18).

J narrates that one day when Moses saw an Egyptian beating a Hebrew he killed him and hid him in the sand (Exod 2:11-12). Dtr^2 exculpates Moses by constructing another identical incident (Exod 2:13-14) that uses forensic language (2:13 *rāšāᶜ*), refers to the law (cp. Exod 21:12-27), and makes Moses its interpreter (2:14 *šōpēṭ*).

J narrates that Yahweh descended on mount Sinai in a cloud, declared the name and attributes of Yahweh and made a covenant with Moses and Israel (Exod 34:5-7, 10-12a, 14, 19,

20b, 22, 24, 27). Dtr[2] revises the narrative to include the decalogue and the story of Israel's rebellions (34:1-4, 8-9, 12b, 13, 15-18, 20a, 21, 23, 25-26, 28). It repeats J's confession that Yahweh forgives guilt and sin (34:9b[b] = 34:7a) but applies it to the story of the golden calf (34:8-9; cf. Exod 32:9, 30-35; 33:3, 5, 16). It repeats J's prohibition of a covenant with the inhabitants of the land (34:15a = 34:12a) but adds redundant warnings against intermarriage, the worship of other gods, and idolatry (34:15b-17). It revises J's festal calendar by repeating some of its key words (34:18, 20a, *ḥag*, *peṭer*), by filling its laws with iteration (34:18, 21, 25, 26b). It has the writing of the words that J prescribes (34:28b[a] = 34:27) but it identifies the words of the covenant with its own decalogue (34:28b[b]) and concludes with a sentence that is marked by balance and repetition (34:28): Moses was with Yahweh forty days and forty nights, he did not eat food and he did not drink water, and he wrote the words of the covenant, the ten words.

J narrates that the earth opened and swallowed Dathan and Abiram and their households and all their possessions (Num 16:25a, 27b-32a, 33a, 34). Dtr[2] extends their fate to Korah and the other rebels (16:25b-27a, 32b, 33b, 35) by repeating J's mention of their tents (16:26 = 16:27b; cp. 16:24, 27a) and of all that belonged to them (16:26 = 16:30, 33a), and then includes a variant for each stage in the punishment described by J (16:32b, 33b, 35).

J narrates that Israel defeated Sihon, king of the Amorites, and lived in his land (Num 21:21-24). Dtr[2] makes Sihon the king of Heshbon, includes the capture of Jazer, and adds the defeat of Og, king of Bashan (Num 21:25-35). To do this Dtr[2] revises J's statement that Israel occupied the land of the Amorites to say that Israel captured their cities, that is, Heshbon and its environs (21:25 = 21:24). Then Dtr[2] explains that Heshbon was the city of Sihon (21:26a), repeats that the Arnon was the border of his land (21:26b = 21:24), and then proves this interpretaion by quoting the song of Heshbon (21:27-30).[105]

J narrates that Balak the son of Sippor summoned Balaam to curse Israel (Num 22:2, 5-6). Dtr[2] identifies him as the king of Moab and makes the Midianites his allies (22:1, 3-4). It repeats his name and says that he was the king of Moab at that time (22:4b), repeats the name Moab three more times (22:3-4a), and emphasizes Moab's fear of Israel by affirming it twice, once in its own language (22:3a; cp. Deut 1:17; 18: 22: I Sam 18:15), once in the language of P (22:3b = Exod 1: 12b).

Dtr^2 uses this pattern to revise the J text without disrupting its narrative thrust. The revisions correct J or relate it to the other sources or give it contemporary and paradigmatic significance. Their language blends them into the source, but the pattern is obtrusive and gives precedence to Dtr^2's ideas and interpretation.

IV. Interests

The principal distinguishing features of the Dtr^2 history are its materials, topics and ideas. The sources were satisfied with a partial and restricted interpretation of the history. J told of the journey and marvelous happenings that led to Israel's settled and separate existence. Dtr^1 narrated the fulfillment of Israel's ideals and aspirations under David and his successors. P retold the story as the fulfillment of promises that God made in the beginning. E emphasized divine guidance and providence. But Dtr^2 wrote a comprehensive and systematic history to demonstrate Israel's distinction from the other nations of the world, to explain the reasons for its dissolution, and to establish the principles of its survival.

A. Materials. Dtr^2's distinctive materials pertain to ethnography. The history regards Israel as one of the nations of the world, describes its origin and organization, defines its boundaries and characteristics, separates it from aborginal peoples, and distinguishes it from the other nations. For instance:

1. Dtr^2 includes references to Assyria, Babylonia, and Egypt that seem to be intrusive in their separate contexts but that are consistent with its geography of the world and contribute to its historical purpose. The garden of Eden is the center of the world and the source of four rivers that encircle

Ethiopia and Egypt and define the boundaries of Assyria and Babylonia (Gen 2:10-14). Ishmael married an Egyptian and his descendents settled between Havilah and Shur, an area that is near Egypt and on the way to Assyria (Gen 21:21; 25:18). Ethiopia and Egypt, Babylon and Assyria, are bound by genealogical ties, are related to the Canaanites and other nations, and are distinguished from the Hebrews (Gen 10:8-19, 21, 24-30; Num 24:22, 24). Abraham was part of the great migrations from Babylon (Gen 11:8a, 9a), lived in Egypt (Gen 12:10-20), and went to war against the kings of Mesopotamia (Gen 14). Israel sojourned in Egypt but was never supposed to return there (Deut 17:16; 28:68).[106] Samaria was exiled to Assyria (II Kgs 17:6). Jerusalem was deported to Babylon (II Kgs 24:10-16; 25:1-12).

2. Dtr^2 portrays Abraham as a contemporary of the aboriginals of Transjordan (Gen 14:5-6) and describes a time when Canaanites and Perizzites lived in the land (Gen 12:6b; 13:7b), before Mamre, Eschol and Aner became place names (Gen 14:13), when Eliezer of Damascus was his heir (Gen 15:2). It calls the earliest heros the Nephilim and considers them the ancestors of the giants who lived in the land before Israel and the nations.[107] It knows the origin of nations (Gen 19:30-38), the explanation of place names[108] and personal names,[109] the origin of customs and occupations,[110] reasons for ritual practice,[111] the relative antiquity of cities (Num 13:22b), variants of personal and proper names,[112] and the names and characteristics of things.[113]

3. Dtr^2 thinks of Israel as the sons of Jacob,[114] refers to them systematically as the sons of Israel,[115] considers them a federation of tribes and describes their peculiar tribal relationships.[116] It records their birth, distributes them among Jacob's wives and paramours, and explains their names.[117] It repeats the list to emphasize their genealogical distribution,[118] and uses the list to characterize them as a group,[119] to explain their military organization,[120] and describe their partition of the land.[121] It is preoccupied with the Transjordanian tribes,[122] singles out the tribe of Levi,[123] and consistently separates Judah from the kingdom of Israel.[124] It is familiar with tribal organization,[125] stresses the authority

of the tribal elders,[126] describes the alignment of the tribes in the era of the conquest (Judg 1-21), and gives legitimate kingship a tribal foundation.[127]

4. Dtr^2's geographical references are detailed and systematic. Cain lived in the land of Nod (Gen 4:16). Bela was renamed Zoar because of its size (Gen 14:8; 19:15-23). Isaac lived at Beerlahairoi, between Qadesh and Bered (Gen 16: 14; 25:11). The territory of the Canaanites is described by listing its border towns and by giving directions to the towns where Abraham and Lot lived (Gen 10:19). Dtr^2 knows the route from Egypt to the plains of Moab (Num 33), the distance from Horeb to Qadesh (Deut 1:1), the precise borders of the land (Num 34:1-12; Josh 22; I Kgs 5:1-5), tribal boundaries (Josh 13-21), the location of Sihon's kingdom (Josh 12:2-5) and the extent of the conquest (Josh 12-13; Judg 1). Dtr^2 describes the land (Deut 6:10-11; 8:7-9; 11:8-12), has detailed directions for getting to Shechem (Deut 11:30) or Shiloh (Judg 21:19) and knows the exact location of battles (Josh 8:12-13; I Sam 13: 16-18; 17:1), the towns captured by Ben Hadad (I Kgs 15:20), and the nations that were defeated by Assyria and resettled in Samaria (II Kgs 17:24; 18:34).

5. Dtr^2 distinguishes Israel from the other nations by describing the hostilities that existed between them. It coined the expression "enemies on all sides",[128] and has a basic antipathy for the Canaanites and Amorites.[129] It introduces the Ammonites and Moabites and makes them traditional foes (Gen 19:30-38; II Kgs 24:2). It considers Amalek and the Philistines typical enemies of the early monarchy.[130] It disagrees with the favorable attitude of the sources and describes conflicts with Midian[131] and Edom.[132] It disparages Egypt,[133] considers the Aramaeans inveterate enemies (II Kgs 13:5), and portrays Assyria and Babylonia as the inevitable instruments of divine punishment.[134] Only Hiram of Tyre, Joram of Hamath, and the Queen of Sheba are exempted from this policy for their contributions to the temple and the royal palace.[135]

B. Topics. Dtr^2 is also distinguished from the sources by its concern for the law, systems and institutions. It records legal and ritual codes and applies their principles to particular situations. It indulges in lists, constructs chronologies, uses calendars, and notices schedules. It is preoccupied with justice and the courts, familiar with religious institutions, and critical of political power. For instance:

1. Dtr^2 corrected the E law code by inserting the decalogue (Exod 20:2-21:1), property laws (Exod 22:9-19), legislation on the festivals (Exod 23:17-19), and exhortations against mingling with the nations (Exod 23:23-25a, 31b-33). It composed a complete revision of the code (Deut 4-30) to comment on Dtr^1's law of centralization. It mentions some particular instances of the law's observance,[136] considers Abraham the model of perfect obedience,[137] recommends Joshua, David, Hezekiah and Josiah for their fidelity,[138] and explains the dissolution of the nation by its disregard for the law (II Kgs 17:7-23). It applies the laws forbidding intermarriage with the inhabitants of the land in the stories of Rebeccah and Dinah (Gen 24, 34), laws of marriage in the story of Judah and Tamar (Gen 38), prohibitions of theft and restrictions on corporate guilt in the story of Joseph and his brothers (Gen 44:16-17), laws against assault and murder in the story of Moses (Exod 2:13-14), laws governing authentic prophecy in the stories of Moses and Balaam (Exod 4:15; Num 22:35), the law of the ban in the defeat of the southern Canaanites (Num 21:1-3), the law prohibiting foreign alliances in the story of Baal Peor (Num 25:1-5), the law of circumcision in the story of the conquest (Josh 5:2-7), regulations concerning the blowing of trumpets in the capture of Jericho (Josh 6:3-6), the law of centralization in defining the boundaries of Yahweh's land (Josh 22), the stipulations of the decalogue in telling the stories of the judges (Judg 2:11-15), the rules to be observed by the judiciary in describing the behaviour of Samuel's sons (I Sam 8:3), the law of centralization in its evaluation of the kings, and the book of the law in its account of the reign of Josiah (II Kgs 22-23).

2. Dtr^2 is concerned with the origin of worship (Gen 4:26; 12:8b) and its proper conduct (Gen 8:20-22). It mentions holy places,[139] altars,[140] shrines,[141] artifacts,[142] offerings and sacrifice,[143] the names of the gods,[144] and divine epithets.[145] It describes the plan and construction of the tent of meeting,[146] the organization of the camp (Num 1-10),

the building, restoration, desecration and destruction of the Jerusalem temple.[147] It prescribes rituals of ordination,[148] orders of service,[149] offerings (Num 28-29), and occasional rites.[150] It includes anecdotes and stories that revolve around the application of ritual prescriptions. The sacrifice of Noah observes the required distinction between clean and unclean animals (Gen 8:20-22). The story of Cain and Abel and the covenant with Noah illustrate the laws prohibiting the eating and shedding of blood (Gen 4:10-12; 9:2-6). The story of Melchizedek elaborates on the ritual of tithes (Gen 14:18-20). The story of Hamor and Shechem is constructed around the law of circumcision (Gen 34). The climax of the plagues in Egypt is reached in the interpretation of Passover (Exod 11:1-8; 12:7, 12-27, 29-36; 13:1-16). The exodus concludes with a song of praise (Exod 15). The story of the manna illustrates the observance of the sabbath (Exod 16:16-34). The exclusion of the people from the theophany on Sinai is based on the laws governing priestly access to the holy things (Exod 19:21-25). The rebellion of Korah applies the same laws to a traditional story of conflict (Num 16:1-11, 15-24, 25b-27a, 32b, 33b, 35). The capture of Jericho depends on the procession of the ark and the ritual blowing of trumpets (Josh 6). The rejection of Saul for sacrificing at Gilgal was anticipated when Samuel offered him the priestly portion (I Sam 9:24). The downfall of the kingdom of Israel was determined by the ritual offences committed by Jeroboam (I Kgs 12:30-33).

3. Dtr[2] has genealogies (Gen 35:16-26) and lists of kings (Gen 36:31-39), of tribal leaders (Num 1:5-16; 13:4-16; 34:16-29), of cities (Num 32:34-38; Deut 4:41-43), encampments (Num 33), provisions (I Kgs 5:2-3), booty (Num 31:32-41), blessings and curses (Deut 27:15-26; 28:1-69). It develops a chronological system for the time between the exodus and the building of the temple.[151] It follows a festal calendar,[152] and is particularly interested in the sabbath and its justification,[153] in the feast of Unleavened Bread and its relation to Passover,[154] and in the offering of the first-born and its connection with the status of the Levitical order.[155] It marks the passage of time,[156] observes the seasons,[157] notes the time of day,[158] has a detailed chronology of the monarchy, and knows the precise dates for the fall of Samaria and the destruction

of Jerusalem.[159]

4. Dtr^2 describes the constitution of the courts,[160] and the possibility of recourse to the king[161] or to divine justice.[162] It admires the law (Deut 4:5-8), considers it Israel's distinguishing feature (Deut 6:25; 9:4-6), encourages its observance, and defends its strict enforcement.[163]

5. Dtr^2 describes the consecration of priests (Exod 28-29, 39; Lev 8-10), defines their rights and obligations (Num 3-8, 16-18; Deut 10:8-9), provides them with an enduring succession (Num 25:10-13; I Sam 2:27-36), and ascribes to individual priests, from Aaron to Hilkiah, a dominant role in the history of the nation. It traces prophetic succession to Moses (Deut 18:15-22; 34:10-12), gives the prophets decisive political power,[164] and considers prophecy the definitive interpretation of history.[165] It also applies to those it esteems some priestly or prophetic attribute: Joshua is given charge of the law and fulfills the function of priest and prophet (Josh 1:7-9; 8:30-35); Miriam and Deborah are prophetesses (Exod 15:20; Judg 4:4); Gideon receives a prophetic call and performs some priestly functions (Judg 6:11-24; 8:22-23); Samuel is a prophet, a priest and a judge (I Sam 2-7); Saul is treated like a priest and a judge and is reckoned among the prophets (I Sam 9:24; 10:12; 11:6; 14:48; 19:23-24); David's final words are spoken in standard prophetic form (II Sam 23:1).

6. Dtr^2 is concerned to limit political power. In the early days wars are fought and won by Yahweh[166] and the spoils belong to the victor.[167] In the time of the judges war is turned against the people and leaders are chosen by Yahweh in response to the prayer of the people (Judg 2:11-23). Kings are subject to the law and religious authority (Deut 17:14-20) and are condemned for their transgressions (II Kgs 17:8). Only those are approved who are anointed for a specific task (I Kgs 9:15; II Kgs 9:1-13) or chosen as Yahweh's viceroy.[168]

C. <u>Ideas</u>. Dtr^2 is also distinguished from the sources by its conception of history and its ideas about God and the nation. It makes persuasion and verification integral to the writing of history by constructing arguments and citing sources. It defines the mutuality of Yahweh and Israel and defends it by appealing to typical, traditional, and indisputable arguments. For instance:

1. Dtr^2 argues from anticipation and resumption to the veracity of its interpretation. It includes in the covenant with Abraham a preview of Israel's history (Gen 15:1-6, 12-16) whose gradual accomplishment in the sequel confirms the accompanying promise of the land (Gen 15:7-11, 17-21). It inspires confidence in the promise to Ishmael (Gen 16:7-14) by anticipating his actual career and habitation (Gen 16:12 = 21:20). It gives substance to its interpretation of the exodus by describing it in advance (Exod 3:15-22) and summarizing it afterward (Deut 26:5-11). It has Jacob predict the history of his sons (Gen 49:1) and makes it more plausible by including events that have occurred (Gen 49:3-7) and blessings that will be repeated (Gen 49:25-26; cf. Deut 33:13-16). It predicts the defeat of the nations (Num 24:14-24) and Israel's decline and exile (Deut 4:30; 21:29), and considers that the events confirm the interpretation (Deut 31:20, 29). It uses prophecy and fulfillment to prove a point (I Kgs 12:15; 15:29) and to explain the connection between disparate events in the history (I Kgs 8:20; 16:34; II Kgs 23:16-18; 24:2).

2. Dtr^2 also argues from the reliability of its information to the correctness of its interpretation. Witnesses cannot be denied[169] and Dtr^2 defends its evaluation of the monarchy and its explanation of Israel's downfall by appealing to the witness of Moses,[170] the law (Deut 31:26), history (Deut 31:19, 21), Samuel (I Sam 8:9) and prophecy (II Kgs 17:15). It exhorts and gives assurances that depend on the witness of the people,[171] and it develops arguments whose point consists in grasping the lesson of history.[172]

3. Dtr^2 also verifies its interpretation by mentioning its sources, such as the annals of the kings or other books,[173] or by citing prayers, songs, speeches or sayings. It has Adam cite a legal fiction to define the bond between man and woman (Gen 3:23-24). It records what Yahweh said before limiting human life (Gen 6:3) and before destroying Sodom and Gomorrah (Gen 18:17-21). It quotes Judah's speech to Joseph (Gen 44:18-34) and the Canaanite reaction to the mourning for Jacob (Gen 50:11). It repeats the ritual that accompanied the ark (Num 10:35-36), Yahweh's decision in a difficult legal case (Num 15:35), and oracular responses in time of war (Judg 1:2; II Sam 2:1).

These quotations either corroborate a specific point, summarize the preceding analysis, or elaborate a particular aspect of the interpretation. The song of Heshbon (Num 21: 27-30) proves that Sihon was the king of Heshbon and confirms the idea that Balak was the king of Moab (Num 21:25-26; 22:3-4). Joshua's speeches summarize the problems created by the nations left in the land (Josh 13:1-7; 23; 24). The song of Deborah contains the ballad of Jael and cross-references that substantiate Dtr^2's story of Deborah and Barak (Judg 4).[174] The song of Moses is a verbatim summary of the exodus narrative combined with hymnic affirmations that prove Dtr^2's point on the uniqueness and supremacy of Yahweh.[175] The speeches of Samuel (I Sam 8; 10:17-19; 12) argue that the pattern of distress, supplication and salvation that pertained in Israel's earlier history will not apply in the time of the monarchy (I Sam 8:18; 12:25).

4. Dtr^2 also has other sources that it does not mention but from which it derives information and ideas. It uses the Gilgamesh epic and revises the flood story so that Noah sends out a raven, removes the covering of the ark, and offers sacrifice.[176] It refers to oppression in Egypt as a wound and to the exodus as healing and may derive these ideas from Jeremiah's description of the distress of Jacob.[177] It seems to know Ezekiel's description of the river in Jerusalem[178] and of the guardian cherub in Eden,[179] and his emphasis on sabbath observance in the wilderness.[180]

5. Dtr^2's distinctive ideas about God and the nation are associated with its theory of law and covenant. The covenant is the decalogue[181] interpreted in the book of the law.[182] It defines the mutuality of Yahweh and Israel (Deut 26:17-19), establishes a correlation between the uniqueness of Yahweh and the distinctiveness of the people (Deut 4:32-40; 7:6-11), determines that other gods are idols and consigns the nations that worship them to destruction (Deut 6:14; 9:4-6; 12:29-31; 29:15-28).

The primacy of the law is affirmed from the beginning of the history and is proved by the effects of disobedience. Disobedience provoked the curses in the garden of Eden (Gen 3:14-19). Violation of the covenant and the worhsip of other gods inevitably inspires the anger of Yahweh and leads to destruction.[183] The final collapse of the nation, consequently, proves the validity of the covenant and argues for continued obedience to the law.[184]

Dtr^2's argument for the uniqueness of Yahweh is the exodus. The plagues in Egypt demonstrate the power of Yahweh[185] and the exclusiveness of Israel.[186] The exodus proves that there is no nation like Israel and that Yahweh alone is God (Deut 4:32-40; 7:6-11). This unique relationship is confirmed by Yahweh's transcendence[187] and accessibility to prayer and prophetic intercession.[188]

Dtr^2's argument for the exclusiveness of Israel is based on the promises to the patriarchs. The exodus (Deut 7:8), the conquest (Deut 6:19; 9:5), the covenant (Deut 26:18-19; 28:9; 29:12), and the possession of the land (Deut 6:10) were promised to Abraham (cf. Gen 12:7; 13:14-17) as his reward for obedience (Gen 15:1-6; 18:17-19; 26:2-5, 23-24). The promises are assembled in a covenant (Gen 15:1-21; 22:15-18) that is transferred to Isaac (Gen 26:2-5, 23-24) and Jacob (Gen 28:13-15; 32:10-13; 48:3-4). It is this covenant that establishes the choice of Israel as Yahweh's people (Deut 4:37; 10:15), that insures the fidelity of Yahweh (Deut 4:31; 9:27; 13:18), and that explains the epithet "God of Israel".[189]

Chapter 6

THE Ps SUPPLEMENT

After the completion of the Dtr^2 history the Pentateuch was formed by the inclusion of a legislative supplement that interprets and revises the ritual laws promulgated by Dtr^2 (Lev 1:1-7:38 + 11:46-27:34). It encloses the Dtr^2 story of Aaron's ordination (Lev 8:1-10:45) and isolates it from its sequel in the history (Num 1-36). It was composed on the model of this sequel, beginning like its introduction (Lev 1:1 = Num 1:1), and ending like its conclusion (Lev 27:34 = Num 36:13).

The Ps supplement comprises four parts (Fig 6), each divided into sections and composed of paragraphs, and each containing different and specific references to the Dtr^2 text. The first part (Lev 1-7) is the ritual for the sacrifices that Dtr^2 mentioned in describing the ordination of Aaron and his sons (Lev 8-10). The second part is the Dtr^2 description with a Ps summary and conclusion (Lev 11:46-47). The third part develops the distinction between clean and unclean (Lev 12-15) that Dtr^2 proposed and Ps repeated in its summary (Lev 11:47 = 10:10), and then it elaborates on other topics that were mentioned in the ordination of Aaron (Lev 16; cp. Lev 8-10). The last part (Lev 17-27) is a revision of Dtr^2's ritual legislation that draws on the laws of centralization and worship (Deut 12-16), on the sets of curses that conclude the covenant (Deut 27-28), and on the repetitions and iterations of these materials in the Dtr^2 history (Num 5, 15, 28-29).

This supplement legitimates its version of the legislation by alluding to its Dtr^2 context but its interests are exclusively juridical and not historical. For instance, it does not use the narrative formula (*wyhy*) to open paragraphs. Similarly, it repeats items from the history (e.g. Lev 16:1-5 = Lev 8:1-9; 10:1-7) but without regard for their chronological or narrative sequence. Or, it copies Dtr^2 in proposing an oracular origin for some legislation (Lev 24:10-23; cp. Num 15:32-36) but it omits Dtr^2's geographical and temporal references and uses the legislation as a pretext for introducing related materials. Or, again, it relies on various Dtr^2 texts for its assemblage of curses (Lev 26) but it omits all the descriptive historical allusions, ignores the covenant, and includes blessings that accrue to the observance of the sabbath year (Lev 26: 34-35; cp. Lev 25).

Each part of the legislation is distinguished from the others by the subject it treats and by its concluding summary.[190] Each section begins with the formula of address ("Yahweh spoke to Moses") and ends with a systematic or synthetic presentation of the law.[191] The first three parts comment on the story of Aaron's ordination and conclude with a section (Lev 16) that both refers to the story and also recapitulates their interest in atonement. The last part comments on Dtr^2's ritual legislation and ends with a section on vows and holy things (Lev 27) that Dtr^1 had mentioned (Deut 12:26) but that Dtr^2 did not include under the law of centralization (cf. Num 6, 30).[192]

The first section of the last part (Lev 17-18) begins by repeating Dtr^2's interpretation that the killing of animals is sacrificial (Deut 12:6, 11, 15, 21, 27) but it diverges from Dtr^2 in not permitting any exception to the law of centralization (Lev 17:1-9; cp. Deut 12:15, 21-25). It agrees with Dtr^2 in prohibiting the shedding and eating of blood (Lev 17:4, 10-14; Gen 9:2-6) but it extends Dtr^2's ruling on the eating of dead animals to include the sojourner (Lev 17:15-16; cp. Deut 14:21a). It follows Dtr^2 in thinking that the law of centralization is meant to exclude false worship (Lev 17:7; Deut 12: 1-3) and the abominable practices of the nations (Lev 18:1-5, 21, 24-30; Deut 12:29-31) but it also quotes Ezekiel (Lev 18: 5 = Ezek 20:11) and develops Dtr^2's curses against sexual deviation into a catalogue of sexual offences (Lev 18:6-23; Deut 27:20-22).

The second section (Lev 19-20) begins with references to the decalogue (Lev 19:3-4, 11-12; Deut 5:8, 11, 12-16, 19-20) and with allusions to the introduction to Dtr^2's dietary laws (Lev 19:1-2; Deut 14:2). It repeats these allusions (Lev 19:27-28), refers to the conclusion to Dtr^2's dietary laws (Lev 19:33-34; 20:25-26; Deut 14:21), and emphasizes again the exclusion of the abominable practices of the nations (Lev 20:

23-24; Deut 12:29-31). Its concern for the holiness of the people and their separation from the nations is the enveloping context (Lev 19:1-4 + 20:23-26) within which Ps revises Dtr^2 laws (Lev 19:13-25, 35-36), repeats Dtr^2 curses (Lev 19:14; 20:9, 11, 17; Deut 27:15-19), reconsiders sexual offences (Lev 20:10-22), and alludes to Dtr^2's laws against sedition (Lev 19:26b, 31; 20:1-9, 27; Deut 13:1-12; 18:9-14).

The third section (Lev 21-22) concerns the priests, refers to Ezekiel (Lev 21:1-15; Ezek 44:19-25), omits mention of the Levites, and stresses Israel's separation from the nations (Lev 22:31-33).

The fourth section (Lev 23-24) is a revision of Dtr^2's legislation on the festivals (Deut 16; Num 28-29) and of regulations concerning the tent of meeting (Exod 25:31; 27:20-21), concluding with the sentence for blasphemy and its precedents (Lev 24:10-23).

The fifth section (Lev 25-26) is a revision of Dtr^2's laws on the year of release (Deut 15:1-18) that extends them to the jubilee year, and a rewriting of Dtr^2's blessings and curses (Deut 28) that depicts the benefits of the patriarchal covenant as the sabbaths of the land (Lev 26).

The last section (Lev 27) applies to vows the rules that Dtr^2 prescribed for the census (Lev 27:1-8; Exod 30:11-16), and reviews the earlier legislation on tithes (Lev 27:30-33; Deut 14:22-27), first-born animals (Lev 27:26-27; Deut 15:19-23) and holy things (Lev 27:14-25; Deut 12:26-27) that Dtr^2 did not include in the laws of centralization.

The Ps legal supplement was grafted onto the Dtr^2 legislation and is extraneous to the Dtr^2 history. Its proper context is the Chr history that reevaluated Dtr^2 and gave the Pentateuch its final coherence.[193]

CONCLUSION

Noth's theory that the Dtr history was composed by one author from written sources and never revised is substantially correct, but the literary and historical assumptions that he maintained instead of verifying the theory are wrong. The author of the history is Dtr^2. The written sources were not fragments transmitted and preserved for their antiquarian interest but the story of the nation interpreted and augmented by generations of historians. The Dtr^2 history is not an editorial compilation of materials but the culmination of an eminent Israelite literary and historiographic tradition (Fig 7).

The successive versions of the history were composed as commentaries on a text. The history composed by J had some specifically Israelite sources and materials but found its precedents in Assyrian, Aramaean, and Canaanite literature. The Dtr^1 history was inspired by J and included legal and annalistic materials of special interest to the Judaean monarchy. The P history confronted and nationalized the sources that J used and introduced the exclusive attitudes that became typical of all the later literature. The E history described regional differences and the complexity of the nation. Dtr^2 composed a universal history filled with research and diverse viewpoints that proved the coincidence of national and theocratic ideals.

The history is complete and coherent. It is composed of paragraphs, sections, episodes, chapters, parts and books. Paragraphs are grammatically distinct, mark the progress of the narrative, and give each work its basic integrity. Each successive composition is continuous with its antecedents. Nothing is excluded and everything enters into a progressively more complex system of relationships. The involvement of the final version contributes to its fascination and makes it unique in the history of Israelite literature.

NOTES

1. *Üs*, 3-12; *ÜP*, 2.

2. *Üs*, 6-12; A. D. H. Mayes, *The Story of Israel between Settlement and Exile. A Redactional Study of the Deuteronomistic History*, London: SCM, 1983, 1-8.

3. *Üs*, 87-90.

4. H.-D. Hoffmann, *Reform und Reformen. Untersuchungen zu einem Grundthema der deuteronomistischen Geschichtsschreibung* [ATANT, 66], Zurich: Theologischer Verlag, 1980, 15-21.

5. *Üs*, 4-6; Mayes, *The Story of Israel*, 4-7.

6. *Üs*, 95-100; *Das Buch Josua* [HAT, 7], Tübingen: J. C. B. Mohr (Paul Siebeck), 1953; *Könige* [BKAT, IX/1], Neukirchen-Vluyn: Neukirchener Verlag, 1968.

7. Mayes, *The Story of Israel*, 8-21.

8. Hoffman (*Reform und Reformen*) avoided Noth's mistakes, was careful to distinguish between literary analysis and historical reconstruction, and demonstrated the unity of the Dtr history of religious reform. The Dtr history envisaged in Noth's theory is designated Dtr^2 in the following analysis to indicate that it derives its basic scope and structure from an earlier version (Dtr^1). This adapts the theory of two versions developed by F. M. Cross (see n. 28, below) to confirm Noth's theory that the author of the history used written sources.

9. *ÜP*; *A History of Pentateuchal Traditions*, trans., B. W. Anderson, Englewood Cliffs: Prentice-Hall Inc., 1972, xiii-xxxii.

10. *ÜP*, 1-4; R. Polzin, "Martin Noth's 'A History of Pentateuchal Traditions'," *BASOR* 221 (1976) 113-120. In Noth's theory tradition is an historical surd. It is not a literary value and it resists literary analysis. It merely expresses the conviction that history is a continuous transmission of historical data generated by historical fact. The J source, for instance, has historical value only because of some uninterrupted but totally imaginary connection with the facts it records. In my analysis, however, tradition is both literary and historical. The literary tradition is the sequence of text and commentary. The historical tradition is the development of interpretation.

11. *ÜP*, 40-44; C. Conroy, "Hebrew Epic: Historical Notes and Critical Reflections," *Bib* 61 (1980) 1-30; F. M. Cross, "The Epic Traditions of Early Israel: Epic Narrative and the Reconstruction of Early Israelite Institutions," R. E. Friedman, ed., *The Poet and the Historian. Essays in Literary and Historical Biblical Criticism*, Chico, CA: Scholars, 1983, 13-39; J. Van Seters, *In Search of History. Historiography in the Ancient World and the Origins of Biblical History*, New Haven: Yale University, 1983, 8-31.

12. *ÜP*, 7-40.

13. R. Rendtorff, "Der 'Jahwist' als Theolge? Zum Dilemma der Pentateuchkritik," *VTS* 28 (1975) 158-166; *Das überlieferungsgeschichtliche Problem des Hexateuch* [BZAW, 147], Berlin: Walter de Gruyter, 1977; "Genesis 15 im Rahmen der theologischen Bearbeitung der Vätergeschichten," R. Albertz *et al* eds., *Werden und Wirken des Alten Testaments. Festschrift für Claus Westermann zum 70. Geburtstag*, Neukirchen-Vluyn: Neukirchener Verlag, 1980, 74-81; "Jakob in Bethel. Beobachtungen zum Aufbau und zur Quellenfrage in Gen 28:10-22," *ZAW* 94 (1982) 511-523; J. Van Seters, "Recent Studies on the Pentateuch: A Crisis in Method," *JAOS* 99 (1979) 663-673.

14. H. H. Schmid, *Der sogenannte Jahwist. Beobachtungen und Fragen zur Pentateuchforschung*, Zurich: Theologischer Verlag, 1976; "Auf der Suche nach neuen Perspektiven für die Pentateuchforschung," *VTS* 32 (1981) 375-394; P. Weimar, *Untersuchungen zur Redaktionsgeschichte des Pentateuch* [BZAW, 146], Berlin: Walter de Gruyter, 1977; S. Tengström, *Die Hexateucherzählung. Eine literaturgeschichtliche Studie*, Lund: C. W. K. Gleerup, 1976; H. C. Schmitt, *Die nichtpriesterliche Josephsgeschichte. Ein Beitrag zur neuesten Pentateuchkritik* [BZAW, 154], Berlin: Walter de Gruyter, 1980; "Redaktion des Pentateuch im Geiste der Prophetie. Beobachtungen zur Bedeutung der 'Glaubens'-Thematik innerhalb der Theologie des Pentateuch," *VT* 32 (1982) 170-189; R. E. Friedman, "Sacred History and Theology: The Redaction of Torah," R. E. Friedman, ed., *The Creation of Sacred Literature. Composition and Redaction of the Biblical Text*, Berkeley: University of California, 1981, 25-34.

15. The criteria of completeness and continuity eliminate from the J source the excerpts and extraneous elements that have been isolated and used to redate J and redefine its position in the history of Israelite literature: H. Vorländer, *Die Entstehungszeit des jehowistischen Geschichtswerkes*, Bern: Peter Lang, 1978; M. Rose, *Deuteronomist und Jahwist. Untersuchungen zu den Berührungspunkten beider Literaturwerke* [ATANT, 67], Zurich: Theologischer Verlag, 1981.

16. Paragraphs are distinguished grammatically by their opening (*wayhî* / disjunction / consecution) and closing markers (disjunction / consecution), and literarily by the linguistic and stylistic features such as repetition, cadence and assonance, that define their topic or theme; cf. B. Peckham, "The Deuteronomistic History of Saul and David," *ZAW* 97 (1985) [forthcoming].

17. Cf. J. L'Hour, "'Yahweh Elohim'," *RB* 81 (1974) 524-556.

18. Cf. J. P. Fokkelman, *Narrative Art in Genesis. Specimens of Stylistic and Structural Analysis*, Assen: Van Gorcum, 1975, 85-237.

19. Cf. R. A. Oden, Jr., "Divine Aspirations in Atrahasis and in Genesis 1-11," *ZAW* 93 (1981) 197-216.

20. The Dtr[2] version eliminates Lot's wife but saves him to father Moab and Ammon (Gen 19:15-23, 24b, 27b, 29-38).

21. The first three episodes are an original version of the Gilgamesh epic and related sources (cf. E. A. Speiser, *Genesis* [AB, 1], Garden City: Doubleday, 1964, 18-76 *passim*; J. H. Tigay, *The Evolution of the Gilqamesh Epic*, Philadelphia: University of Pennsylvania, 1982). J's familiarity with Assyrian, Phoenician, Aramaean and Greek sources is evident in the story of the revelation to Abraham at Hebron (C. Westermann, *Genesis* [BKAT, I], Neukirchen-Vluyn: Neukirchener Verlag, 1979, 332-335), in the account of the birth of Moses (W. H. Schmidt, *Exodus* [BKAT, II/I], Neukirchen-Vluyn: Neukirchener Verlag, 1974, 49-65), in the descriptions of Yahweh's power (F. M. Cross, *Canaanite Myth and Hebrew Epic*, Cambridge: Harvard University, 1973, 112-169), in the idea of a covenant that is made with a nation and its leader (Exod. 34:10, 27; cf. M. Weinfeld, art., *bĕrît*, G. J. Botterweck - H. Ringgren, eds., *Theologisches Wörterbuch zum Alten Testament*, I, Stuttgart: W. Kohlhammer, 1973, 781-808), and in the story of Balaam (J. Hoftijzer - G. Van Der Kooij, *Aramaic Texts from Deir ᶜAlla*, Leiden: Brill, 1976).

22. J selected material to describe a regular pattern of migration and settlement by an increasingly larger group of herdsmen and shepherds that culminated in Israel's possession of the land. The journey began in the east at Eden and moved gradually westward through Sumer to the land of Canaan with stops at Shechem, Bethel, Hebron and Gerar. Another journey led from Harran to Shechem, Dothan and Gilead. The third led from Egypt to Etham and Sinai in the wilderness, to the Negeb, Hebron and Qadesh, and finally to the land of the Amorites. Strange and wonderful things happen on the journeys, but the settlements are marked by arguments, disagreements, attempts at reconciliation, and the making of covenants. The pattern is also reinforced by the repetition of themes: Abraham and Lot offer the same hospitality to the three visitors; the destruction of Sodom and Gomorrah resembles both the flood (*mṭr*, Gen 7:4a; 19:24a) and Yahweh's theophany on mount Sinai (*kibšān*, Gen 19:28; Exod 19:18ab[a]); there are similarities in the apparitions to Abraham and Moses (*nṣb*, *ᶜbr*, *plᵓ*, *bn*, Gen 18:2-5, 10, 14; Exod 34:5-6, 10, 19, 20b); there is a famine in the time of Isaac and in the time of Jacob (Gen 26:1a[a]b; 41:54b); the command that Abimelek gave his people is like the command that Yahweh gave in the garden (Gen 2:16-17; 3:3; 26:11); both Jacob and Moses meet their prospective brides at a well in a foreign country (Gen 29:4-12; Exod 2:16-21) and both are assaulted by God on their homeward journey (Gen 32:14a, 25b, 27-29; Exod 4:24-26); Isaac's prosperity threatens the Philistines (Gen 26:16-17) as Israel's prosperity threatens the Egyptians (Exod 1:8-11a, 12a).

23 Each episode is self-contained but related in various ways to the others. The cohesion of the fourth episode, for instance, is expressed by the repetition of themes: Jacob is blessed by his father and by God (Gen 27:23, 33; 32:27-29); the rule of primogeniture is ignored by Rebeccah and Jacob (Gen 27:17-23; 29:18, 26); both Isaac and Jacob prosper in an

alien land and then separate from their patron (Gen 26:12-14, 16-17; 32:4-7); Jacob uses deceit both with Isaac and with Laban (Gen 27:17-19, 21-23; 30:35-42). It is related to the preceding episode by its interest in Isaac, to the following episode by its mention of Joseph and Israel (Gen 30:25; 32:29; 37:3a), to the last episode in the history by the theme of blessing (Num 23:11, 20, 25: 24:1, 10), to the first episode by certain similarities between Rebeccah and the forbidden fruit (Gen 2:9, 16-17; 3:3, 6; 26:7, 11), and to the second episode by the similarity between Abimelek and the sons of God (Gen 6:2; 26:7).

24. The narrative action always requires the participation of Yahweh and in every episode except the fifth Yahweh is the ally of the protagonist. In the fifth episode this narrative function is assumed by Joseph who provides food for his brothers and becomes the arbiter of life and death (Gen 42:2, 20; 43:7, 8, 27, 28; 45:3, 26a[a]b, 28; 46:30).

25. The point of the J narrative is the gradual differentiation of the people of Israel from the world and from the nations that surround them. This takes place under the tutelage of Yahweh and is the final destination of the journey (Num 23:9). It becomes particularly evident in the final episode when Yahweh participates in the pattern of migration and settlement (Exod 13:19-20; 14:19b-20, 24, 27b; Num 16:27b-32a, 33a, 34) and makes a covenant with the people to confirm this fact (Exod 34:10, 27; Num 23:18-24; 24:5-6, 8a-9).

26. *ÜS*, 6-10.

27. A. Jepsen, *Die Quellen des Königsbuches*, Halle (Saale): Max Miemeyer, 1953; W. Dietrich, *Prophetie und Geschichte. Eine redaktionsgeschichtliche Untersuchung zum deuteronomistischen Geschichtswerk* [FRLANT, 108], Göttingen: Vandenhoeck & Ruprecht, 1972; T. Veijola, *Die Ewige Dynastie. David und die Entstehung seiner Dynastie nach der deuteronomistischen Darstellung* [Annales Academiae Scientiarum Fennicae, B/193], Helsinki, 1975; *Das Königtum in der Beurteilung der deuteronomistischen Historiographie. Eine redaktionsgeschichtliche Untersuchung* [Annales Academiae Scientiarum Fennicae, B/198], Helsinki, 1977; *Verheissung in der Krise. Studien zur Literatur und Theologie der Exilszeit anhand des 89. Psalms* [Annales Academiae Scientiarum Fennicae, B/220], Helsinki, 1982.

28. F. M. Cross, "The Themes of the Book of Kings and the Structure of the Deuteronomistic History," *Canaanite Myth and Hebrew Epic*, Cambridge: Harvard University, 1973, 274-289; R. E. Friedman, *The Exile and Biblical Narrative. The Formation of the Deuteronomistic and Priestly Works* [HSM, 22], Chico: Scholars Press, 1981; "From Egypt to Egypt: Dtr[1] and Dtr[2]," B. Halpern and J. D. Levenson, eds., *Traditions in Transformation. Turning Points in Biblical Faith*, Winona Lake: Eisenbrauns, 1981, 167-192; R. D. Nelson, *The Double Redaction of the Deuteronomistic History* [JSOTSS, 18], Sheffield: The University of Sheffield, 1981.

29. R. Smend, "Das Gesetz und die Völker. Ein Beitrag zur deuteronomistischen Redaktionsgeschichte," H. W. Wolff, ed., *Probleme biblischer Theologie. Gerhard von Rad zum 70. Geburtstag*, Munich: Chr. Kaiser, 1971, 494-509; R. G. Boling, *Judges* [AB, 6a], Garden City: Doubleday, 1975; *Joshua* [AB, 6], Garden City: Doubleday, 1982; Mayes, *The Story of Israel*, 1983.

30. The literary evidence for the complexity and composite unity of the Dtr history has been analyzed by R. Polzin, *Moses and the Deuteronomist. A Literary Study of the Deuteronomistic History, I: Deuteronomy, Joshua, Judges*, New York: Seabury, 1980. The consistency and coherence of the Dtr interpretation has been demonstrated by Hoffmann, *Reform und Reformen*.

31. The fact that Dtr[1] is the sequel to J and has some of its characteristics but is devoid of the features considered typical of Dtr may explain why the pentateuchal sources have been traced in Josh-II Kgs; cf. O. Eissfeldt, *Einleitung in das Alte Testament*, Tübingen: J. C. B. Mohr (Paul Siebeck), 1964; F. Langlamet, "Josué et les traditions de l'Hexateuque," *RB* 78(1971) 5-17, 161-183, 321-354. The other fragmentary sources proposed for the Pentateuch, such as L (Eissfeldt, *Einleitung*, 258-264) or N (G. Fohrer, *Introduction to the Old Testament*, trans. David E. Green, Nashville: Abingdon, 1968, 159-165), conversely, usually comprise random excerpts from Dtr[2]'s revision of J.

32. The opening words of the history (Deut 1:1a *ʾēlleh haddĕbārîm*; cf. Deut 6:6; 31:1), from this perspective, allude to the closing words of the J covenant on Sinai (Exod 34:27, *haddĕbārîm hāʾēlleh*).

33. The conquest is the subject of J's covenant on Sinai (Exod 34:10-12, 24).

34. Dtr[1] included the J festivals of Weeks and Ingathering under the rubric of tithes on produce (Exod 34:22; Deut 14:22, 25-26), kept the offering of first-born animals (Exod 34:19; Deut 15:19-20), and replaced the dedication of first-born sons with the feast of Passover (Exod 34:20b; Deut 16:2a, 7a). P revised the feast of Passover (Exod 12:1-6, 8-11, 28) and Dtr[2] combined it with the festival of Massot (Exod 12:7, 12-27; Deut 16:1-8).

35. Most of the J text is repeated in the Dtr[1] version: Exod 34:5 in Deut 5:4; 34:7 in 5:9b[b]-10; 34:10 in 7:21; 34:11a in 12:14b; 34:11b-12a in 7:1-2ab[b]; 34:14 in 5:7, 9b[a]; 34:19, 20b in 15:19-20 and 16:2a, 7a, 16b; 34:22 in 14:22, 25-26; 34:24 in 11:23 and 12:20 and 16:16a[a]; and 34:27 in 1:1a and 6:6 and 31:1.

36. Josh 1:1-2 = Deut 31:1-2a, 3a; Josh 1:3-5a = Deut 11:23-25a; Josh 1:5b[b] = Deut 31:6b[b].

37. Josh 3:5b + 10b = Exod 19:10a + 34:10a, 11b; cf. B. Peckham, "The Composition of Josh 3-4," *CBQ* 46 (1984) 413-431.

38. Cf. B. Peckham, "The Deuteronomistic History of Saul and David," *ZAW* 97 (1985) [forthcoming].

39. The specific reason for the exile of Samaria (II Kgs 18:12b *wĕloɔ šamĕᶜû wĕloɔ ᶜāśû*) quotes and negates the people's acceptance of the covenant at Horeb (Deut 5:27 *wĕšāmaᶜnû wĕᶜāśînû*). Trust in Yahweh, conversely, is related to Hezekiah's enactment of the law of centralization (II Kgs 18:22) and to the observance of the Dtr^1 version of the covenant at Horeb.

40. J. Van Seters, *In Search of History*, 68-76.

41. The Dtr^1 story of Hezekiah (Fig 2: VIII, 26-30) shows familiarity and a measure of disagreement with Isaiah's oracles. The idea that Yahweh has brought Assyria against Jerusalem (II Kgs 18:25) seems to allude to Isaiah's contention that Assyria is the rod of Yahweh's anger (Isa 10:5-7). The capture of Judaean cities that Dtr^1 mentions (II Kgs 18:13) is the subject of Isaiah's next oracle (Isa 10:27b-32). Isaiah condemns Jerusalem's treaty with Egypt (Isa 28:14-16, 17b-19; 30:1-5) that the Assyrian envoys imply is the basis of Hezekiah's hope (II Kgs 18:21, 23-24; 19:8). Isaiah condemns Jerusalem's lack of trust (Isa 30:15-17) but Dtr^1 emphasizes just the opposite (II Kgs 18:19-22, 29-30).

42. P's function as a commentary and its complete reliance on J has led to the conclusion that P was an edition of the Pentateuch rather than one of its sources (cf. F. M. Cross, "The Priestly Work," *Canaanite Myth and Hebrew Epic*, 293-325). That P, in an early edition, was a response to Dtr^1, has been argued by R. E. Friedman, *The Exile and Biblical Narrative*, 44-119.

43. K. Elliger, "Sinn und Ursprung der priesterlichen Geschichtserzählung," *ZTK* 49 (1952) 121-143; W. Brueggemann, "The Kerygma of the Priestly Writers," *ZAW* 84 (1972) 397-414.

44. J.F. Wimmer, "Tradition Reinterpreted in Exod 6, 2-7, 7," *Augustinianum* 7 (1967) 405-418; N. Lohfink, "Die priesterschriftliche Abwertung der Tradition von der Offenbarung des Jahwenamens an Mose," *Bib* 49 (1968) 1-8.

45. The land is J's principal topic and its possession is the subject of a promise (Exod 3:8), a covenant (Exod 34:10, 11b), and an oath (Num 14:16, 23). P systematized the covenant and extended the notion of promise to include matters such as progeny and prosperity that J had simply narrated (Gen 9:1, 9-17; 17:1-27). P also borrowed Dtr^1's idea that dynastic succession would insure the maintenance of the covenant and possession of the land but used it to describe the stability and continuity of the promise to Abraham, Isaac, Jacob and the sons of Israel (Exod 2:24; 6:3-9). Cf. C. Westermann, *Die Verheissungen an die Väter. Studien zur Vätergeschichte*, Göttingen: Vandenhoeck & Ruprecht, 1976; J. A. Emerton, "The Origin of the Promises to the Patriarchs in the Older Sources of the Book of Genesis," *VT* 32 (1982) 14-32; H. Seebass, "Gehörten Verheissungen zum ältesten Bestand der Väter-Erzählungen?," *Bib* 64 (1983) 189-210.

46. Exod 40:17-19, 35b-37: Num 10:11-12; 12:16b. The different interpretations of the temple given by Dtr[1] and by P are related to their different understandings of the land: Dtr[1]'s notion of centralization had theological significance (e.g. Deut 6:4 *yhwh ᵓeḥād*) but it also had strict partisan implications; P's wilderness sanctuary was an adaptation of J's theory of Yahweh's concomitance to its own national interests.

47. Noth, *ÜP*, 17. N. Lohfink ("Die Priesterschrift und die Geschichte," *VTS* 29 [1978] 189-225) observed that P is more concerned with evaluating history than it is in recounting a sequence of historical events. P knows and corrects Dtr[1] and offers an alternative interpretation of J that counteracts Dtr[1]'s emphasis on the covenant, the conquest, and the Davidic dynasty. It comments on J by writing another version of the history that is conspicuous, single-minded and consistent, but deliberately constructed to weight and balance the original narrative.

48. In most cases J and P are consecutive and the paragraphing of each is unchanged by their combination. But in five instances (Fig 3: IV, 4; V, 3, 20, 35, 40) there is elision of the J and P paragraphs; and in another instance (Fig 3: V, 42) the P paragraphing supposes the presence of the Dtr[1] narrative (Deut 1:1a; 5:1a[a], 2-3; 31:1, 2a, 3a, 6) and has been modified by the insertion of Dtr[2] texts.

49. R. R. Wilson, "The Old Testament Genealogies in Recent Research," *JBL* 94 (1975) 169-189; *Genealogy and History in the Biblical World*, New Haven: Yale University, 1977. The genealogies have the same historiographic function in P that the king-lists have in Dtr[1] (cf. n. 40, above). The *tôlĕdôt* formula opens a chapter (Gen 5:1a; 10:1; 25:12), closes a chapter when the J variant follows (Gen 2:4a; 37:2a[a]), or marks the transition from chronology to the particular topic that P intends to develop (Gen 6:9; 11:10, 27; 25:19; 36:1).

50. The cosmological perspective of P's creation account has affinities with the *Enuma Elish* and western cosmogonies and distinguishes P from the humane interests that J shares with *Gilgamesh*, *Atrahasis*, and the later epics: cf. Westermann, *Genesis*, 24-97; F. M. Cross, "The 'Olden Gods' in Ancient Near Eastern Creation Myths," F. M. Cross *et al* eds., *Magnalia Dei. The Mighty Acts of God. Essays on the Bible and Archaeology in Memory of G. Ernest Wright*, Garden City: Doubleday, 1976, 329-338.

51. S. E. McEvenue, *The Narrative Style of the Priestly Writer*, Rome: Biblical Institute Press, 1971; B. W. Anderson, "A Stylistic Study of the Priestly Creation Story," G. W. Coats - B. O. Long, eds., *Canon and Authority. Essays in Old Testament Religion and Theology*, Philadelphia: Fortress, 1977, 148-162.

52. Cf. M. Weinfeld, "Sabbath, Temple and the Enthronement of the Lord - The Problem of the Sitz im Leben of Genesis 1:1-2:3," A. Caquot - M. Delcor, eds., *Mélanges bibliques et*

orientaux en l'honneur de M. Henri Cazelles [AOAT, 212], Neukirchen-Vluyn: Neukirchener Verlag, 1981 501-512.

53. S.E. McEvenue, *The Narrative Style of the Priestly Writer*, 22-89; C. Westermann, *Genesis*, 532-546.

54. P replaces the semi-divine status of Adam in J with Noah's fidelity to God (Gen 6:9 - 5:22, 24), shifts the blame from human pretensions to the crimes that ruin the created order, and eliminates any trace of divine irrationality by alluding to the judgement pronounced in a saying of Amos (cf. R. Smend, "'Das Ende is gekommen'. Ein Amoswort in der Priesterschrift," J. Jeremias - L. Perlitt, *Die Botschaft und die Boten. Festschrift für H. W. Wolff zum 70. Geburtstag*, Neukirchen-Vluyn: Neukirchener Verlag, 1981, 67-72.

55. P's revision demonstrates familiarity with the standard Babylonian flood story in the construction of the ark, in the selective preservation of creatures, and in the restoration of the created order (Gen 6:14-16, 19-20; 9:1, 9-16; Westermann, *Genesis*, 542-544, 562-566).

56. P's flood story repeats the language and ideas of its creation account. It begins with a summary of creation (Gen 5:1-2), repeats the list of creatures from the account (Gen 6:19b-20a; 7:14-16, 21; 8:17; 9:10), uses the same cosmology (Gen 7:11, 18-20; 8:2, 14) and calendar (Gen 7:11, 24; 8:3, 13-14), repeats the original blessing (8:17; 9:1) and has the same concern for the provision of food (6:21).

57. C. Westermann, "Gen 17 und die Bedeutung von 'Berit'," *TLZ* 101 (1976) 161-170; W. Gross, "Bundeszeichen und Bundesschluss in der Priesterschrift," *TTZ* 87 (1978) 98-115.

58. M. Oliva, "Las revelaciones a los patriarcas en la historia sacerdotal," *Bib* 55 (1974) 1-14; P. Weimar, "Aufbau und Struktur der priesterschriftlichen Jakobsgeschichte," *ZAW* 86 (1974) 174-203; M. Fishbane, "Composition and Structure in the Jacob Cycle (Gen 25:19-35:22)," *JJS* 26 (1975) 15-38.

59. P's literary techniques are analyzed in detail by S. E. McEvenue, *The Narrative Style of the Priestly Writer*; "Word and Fulfillment: A Stylistic Feature of the Priestly Writer," *Semitics* 1 (1970) 104-110; "The Style of a Building Instruction," *Semitics* 4 (1974) 1-9; " A Comparison of Narrative Styles in the Hagar Stories," *Semeia* 3 (1975) 64-80. The relationship that McEvenue noticed between the style of P and modern children's literature is due to P's interest in argument and explanation, its reliance on the primary logical principles of identity and distinction, and its systematic use of periodicity and binary opposition.

60. J. L. Ska, "Les plaies d'Egypte dans le récit sacerdotal (Pg)," *Bib* 60 (1979) 23-35; "La sortie d'Egypte (Exod 7-14) dans le récit sacerdotal (Pg) et la tradition prophétique," *Bib* 60 (1979) 191-215.

61. Cp. Deut 16:2a, 7a. P gives the date of Passover, the ritual of the festival and its rationale, and disagrees with Dtr[1] on every point, viz. that it is a sacrifice, that oxen or sheep could be offered, that they should be boiled and eaten at the temple.

62. A. W. Jenks, *The Elohist and North Israelite Traditions* [SBLMS, 22], Missoula: Scholars, 1977; J. F. Craghan, "The Elohist in Recent Literature," *BTB* 7 (1977) 23-35.

63. There are thirty-seven instances: Fig 4: I, 1-2, 4-5; II, 1-5, 10, 11, 14, 15; III, 1-3, 5, 6, 9, 13, 14, 17, 18, 20, 21, 24, 25, 30, 33, 34, 35, 36; IV, 2, 4, 12, 33, 34.

64. There are twelve instances: Fig 4: I, 3, 6, 11; II, 8, 12, 16; III, 7, 21, 28; IV, 6, 10, 32.

65. There are five instances: Fig 4: I, 8; II, 6; IV, 8, 32, 36.

66. These include all the laws (Fig 4: IV, 13-32) and fourteen other instances: Fig 4: I, 10; II, 9, 13; III, 8, 19, 22, 23, 27, 29, 32; IV, 1, 5, 9, 11.

67. There are thirteen instances: Fig 4: I, 7, 9; II, 7; III, 4, 10, 11, 12, 15, 16, 31; IV, 3, 7, 36. They usually contain some temporal modifier such as *ʾăḥar haddĕbārîm hāʾēlleh* (Fig 4: I, 8; III, 12, 29), *bāʿēt* (Fig 4: I, 7; II, 7), *kĕhayyôm hazzeh* (Fig 4: III, 10), *miqqēṣ šĕnatayim yāmîm* (Fig 4: III, 15), *babboqer* (Fig 4: III, 16), *mimmoḥŏrat* (Fig 4: IV, 7); or verbal clauses with a temporal nuance such as *kišmoʿ* (Fig 4: II, 4), *kaʾăšer bāʾ* (Fig 4: III, 4), *bĕšallaḥ* (Fig 4: IV, 3), or *kaʾăšer qārab* (Fig 4: IV, 36).

68. Cf. G. W. Coats, "Strife without Reconciliation. A Narrative Theme in the Jacob Traditions," R. Albertz *et al* eds., *Werden und Wirken des Alten Testaments. Festschrift für Claus Westermann zum 70. Geburtstag*, Neukirchen-Vluyn: Neukirchener Verlag, 1980, 82-106; R. Couffignal, "Le songe de Jacob. Approches nouvelles de Genèse 28, 10-22," *Bib* 58 (1977) 342-368; C. Houtman, "What did Jacob See in his Dream at Bethel? Some Remarks on Genesis 28:10-22, *VT* 27 (1977) 337-351; E. Otto, "Jakob in Bethel. Ein Beitrag zur Geschichte der Jakobüberlieferung," *ZAW* 88 (1976) 165-190; A. de Pury, *Promesse divine et légende cultuelle dans le cycle de Jacob. Genesè 28 et les traditions patriarchales*, Paris: Gabalda, 1975; R. Rendtorff, "Jakob in Bethel. Beobachtungen zum Aufbau und zur Quellenfrage in Gen 28:10-22," *ZAW* 94 (1982) 511-523; W. Richter, "Das Gelübde als theologische Rahmung der Jakobsüberlieferungen," *BZ* 11 (1967) 21-52.

69. E's dependence on P is particularly evident in the description of Jacob's escape (Gen 31:18) that borrows ideas and language from the conclusion of P's story of Jacob (cf. Gen:27; 36:6). The story of Jacob's flight from Paddan Aram is also modeled on J's version of the exodus (*brḥ*, Gen 31:20-22, 27; Exod 14:5a) and the covenant on Sinai (*krt bryt*, Gen

31:44, 51-54; Exod 34:10) and by anticipating it lessens its effects.

70. Noth, *ÜP*, 40-44. E had ideas and information of its own that were not derived from its usual historical sources. These can be traced to other literary works (e.g. Exod 3: 13-14: Hos 1:8-9), to recent religious prescription (e.g. Gen 28:22; Amos 4:4; Deut 14:22), or to contemporary interest in the law and its codification (e.g. Exod 21:1-11; Amos 2:6-8).

71. The correspondence between the two parts is concrete and detailed: the genealogy of Adam that culminates in the worship of Yahweh (Fig 5: I, A, 4: Gen 4:26) composes a period with Jacob's worship at Beersheba and the adjunct list of his descendants (5: I, G, 1; Gen 46:1-27); the hostility between Cain and Abel is resolved in the blessing of Ephraim and Manasseh (5: I, A, 3 / G, 3); the relation of God and Adam in the government of the world (5: I, A, 1-3) contrasts with Pharaoh's control of the land and enslavement of his people (5: I, G, 2); likeness to God and the struggle for a lasting life (5: I, A, 1-2) are the polar opposite of the death of Jacob (5: I, G, 4-5) with its explicit distinction between God and Joseph (Gen 50:19).

72. The argument and interpretation of this part are developed in its symmetrical opposite (5: I, E, 1-10; Gen 25-35) that illustrates the blessing and the promise, describes Jacob's sojourn in Mesopotamia, and explains why Isaac did not go to Egypt.

73. N. Lohfink, *Die Landverheissung als Eid. Eine Studie zu Gn 15*, Stuttgart: *KBW*, 1967; L. Perlitt, *Bundestheologie im Alten Testament* [WMANT, 36], Neukirchen-Vluyn: Neukirchener Verlag, 1969, 57-77; R. Rendtorff, "Genesis 15 im Rahmen der theologischen Bearbeitung der Vätergeschichten," R. Albertz *et al* eds., *Werden und Wirken des Alten Testaments*, 1980, 74-81; M. Anbar, "Genesis 15: A Conflation of Two Deuteronomic Narratives," *JBL* 101 (1982) 39-55.

74. The connection between the Levites, the offering of the first-born, and the destruction of the Egyptians is defined by Dtr[2] in Num 3:11-13, 40-51; the connection between Massot and the offering of the first-born in Exod 13:1-16.

75. G. E. R. Lloyd, *Polarity and Analogy. Two Types of Argumentation in Early Greek Thought*, Cambridge: Cambridge University, 1966.

75. B. Peckham, "The Composition of Deuteronomy 5-11," C. L. Meyers - M. O'Connor, eds., *The Word of the Lord Shall Go Forth. Essays in Honor of David Noel Freedman in Celebration of his Sixtieth Birthday*, Winona Lake: Eisenbrauns, 1983, 217-240.

77. C. Carmichael, *The Laws of Deuteronomy*, Ithaca: Cornell University, 1974; S. A. Kaufman, "The Structure of the Deuteronomic Law," *Maarav* 1 (1979) 105-158.

78. B. Peckham, "The Composition of Joshua 3-4," *CBQ* 46 (1984) 413-431.

79. The sixth book (Judges) is the symmetrical opposite of the third (Leviticus-Numbers): it describes the the tribal disintegration that replaced the tribal community in the desert; it demonstrates that rebellion is a violation of the covenant and has uniform and predictable results. The seventh book (Samuel) is the analogue of the second (Exodus): the story of Samuel repeats and refers to the story of Moses and the plagues in Egypt (e.g. I Sam 2:27; 3:7; 6:4-6); the story of Saul refers to the exodus (I Sam 8:8; 10:18; 12:6-8), imitates it by referring to the Israelites as "Hebrews" (I Sam 13-14), and completes it with Saul's war against the Amalekites (I Sam 15; Exod 17); the story of David is engineered by covenants and refers to the covenant on Sinai (II Sam 7:22-24), brings to Jerusalem the ark and the tent that were constructed at Sinai (II Sam 6-7), and is marked by the revolt of Absalom whose ideals reflect the purpose of the judicial reforms instituted by Moses (Exod 18: II Sam 15:1-6). The eighth book (Kings) is the polar opposite of the first (Genesis) and confirms the sequence of events predicted by Deuteronomy: the temple of Solomon is given cosmic significance (I Kgs 7-8), Solomon is comparable to Adam with knowledge of good and evil (I Kgs 3:9), and in his reign the promises to the patriarchs were fulfilled (I Kgs 3:8; 4:20); the history of Jeroboam (I Kgs 12-15) has the geographical references familiar from the story of Jacob (Gen 26-35); and the most obvious resumption occurs at the end of the book and the history when Deuteronomy is reintroduced to substantiate Dtr^2's interpretation (II Kgs 22-23). This interconnectedness of the books is a product of careful organization and a result of consistent historical interpretation. Events do not speak for themselves but illustrate a detailed and comprehensive point of view that is articulated periodically and by analogy. Parts of the argument are summarized from time to time in historical reviews, but Dtr^2's interpretation is inseparable from the repetitive process.

80. D. W. Gooding, "The Composition of the Book of Judges," *ErIsr* 16 (1982) 70*-79*.

81. B. Peckham, "The Deuteronomistic History of Saul and David," *ZAW* 97 (1985) [forthcoming].

82. These two parts are connected in incidental and in substantial ways: the perversion of justice under Samuel's sons resembles Absalom's complaint against David (I Sam 8:1-3; II Sam 15:1-6); the prediction that a king would have a personal bodyguard and a standing army is verified in the reigns of Absalom and David (I Sam 8:11-12; II Sam 15:1; 18:1; cf. I Sam 22:7); Saul and Absalom are singled out of all Israel for their beauty (I Sam 9:2; II Sam 14:25); both reign in the northern kingdom; David laments for both.

83. B. Peckham, "The Deuteronomistic History of Saul and David," *ZAW* 97 (1985) [forthcoming].

84. P. Weimar, *Untersuchungen zur Redaktionsgeschichte des Pentateuch* [BZAW, 146], Berlin: Walter de Gruyter, 1977, 5-55.

85. There are two exceptions: the severity of the famine (Gen 12:10b[b] *kābēd hārā*[c]*āb*) and entrance (*bwɔ*) rather than descent (*yrd*) into Egypt (Gen 12:11a, 14a). But both of these expressions are taken from the other story of Israel's sojourn in Egypt (*r*[c]*b kbd*, Gen 47:4, 13; *bwɔ*, Gen 41:57; 46:6-8, 26-27; 48:5).

86. The promise that Abraham would be a great nation is from P and E (Gen 12:2a[a]; 17:5-6, 20; 46:3), blessing is from the Jacob narrative in J (Gen 12:2-3; 26:12; 27 *passim*), and the contrast between blessing and curse has structural significance in J (Gen 12:3a; 27:29; Num 24:9). Dtr[2] included the idea of a great name (Gen 12:2) and the notion of the family of nations (Gen 12:3; cp. Gen 10:5, 20, 31 = P).

87. The promise of descendants (Gen 13:16) seems intrusive (cf. Westermann, *Genesis*, 210) but it refers to Balaam's first vision (Num 23:10 *mnh* [c]*pr*) and has the same literary setting (Gen 13:14, separation of Abraham from Lot; Num 23:9b, separation of Israel from the nations.). Dtr[2] also refers to P's promise of the land (Gen 13:15 = Gen 17:8) and to the vision of the land that P accords to Moses (Gen 13:17 = Num 27:12; Deut 32:49; 34:4 = Deut 3:27 Dtr[2]).

88. The P covenant mentions the monarchy (Gen 17:6, 16) and Dtr[2]'s version alludes to the covenant with David (Gen 15:4b = II Sam 7:12). Dtr[2] also refers to Dtr[1]'s version of the Sinai covenant (Gen 15:7 = Deut 5:6), to E texts on the Egyptian sojourn (Gen 15:13, 16; cp. Gen 47:13-26; 50:23), and to P texts concerning the death of Abraham (Gen 15:15 = Gen 25:8) and the plagues in Egypt (Gen 15:14 = Exod 7:4).

89. Most of Gen 44:18-34 is taken from the J narrative but some is from E (Gen 44:28-29 = Gen 37:33, 35).

90. Reuben's incest was noted incidentally in the story of Jacob (Gen 49:4 = 36:22); the vendetta of Simeon and Levi was narrated in the story of Dinah (Gen 49:5-7 = 34:25-31); Judah's preeminence is described in part with an image from Joseph's dream (Gen 49:8 = 37:10), and in part with the language of the Balaam oracles (Gen 49:9-10 = Num 23:24; 24:9, 17); the Joseph saying is repeated from the blessing of Moses (Gen 49:25-26 = Deut 33:13, 15).

91. In the Dtr[2] version the plagues separate Israel from the Egyptians (Exod 8:18-19; 9:4-7; 11:7; 12:21-27), give them special status among the people (Exod 3:21, 11:3), and require Pharaoh's submission to Moses (Exod 8:4-9a, 24-27; 12:32) and to Yahweh (Exod 9:13-16, 27-30).

92. Exod 15 has hymnic elements (15:3, 6-8, 11-13, 17-18) that are combined with narrative themes taken from the account in Exod 14 and related texts: 15:1a = Num 21:17; 15:1b-2 =

Exod 3:13; 14:9, 30: 15:4-5 = Exod 13:18; 14:7, 9, 25; 15:9-10 = Exod 14:8a, 9a[a], 21, 28; 15:14-16 = Exod 13:17; 23:27. The final strophe anticipates the conquest and settlement (Exod 15:14-18) and its significance is explained by Dtr² in its revision of the Jericho account (Josh 2-5). Cf. E. Zenger, "Tradition und Interpretation in Exodus 15:1-21," *VTS* 32 (1981) 452-483; B. Halpern, "Doctrine by Misadventure. Between the Israelite Source and the Biblical Historian," R. E. Friedman, ed., *The Poet and the Historian. Essays in Literary and Historical Biblical Criticism*, Chico, CA: Scholars, 1983, 41-73.

93. Lothar Perlitt, *Bundestheologie im Alten Testament* [WMANT, 36], Neukirchen-Vluyn: Neukirchener Verlag, 1969, 167-181. Dtr² combines the standard appellation *bĕnê yiśrā᾽ēl* with the unusual designation *bêt yaᶜăqob* (Exod 19:3; cf. Mic 2:7; Jer 2:4; 5:20; Ezek 20:5); uses the peculiar language of the exodus (Exod 19:4a = Exod 14:31), the wilderness wanderings (Exod 19:4b[a] = Deut 32:11) and the settlement in the holy land (Exod 19:4b[b] = Exod 15:17); uses the language of P to describe fidelity to the covenant (Exod 19:5 *šmr bryt* = Gen 17:9) and the language of E to define obedience (Exod 19:5 *šmᶜ bqwl* = Exod 23:21-22); and redistributes the elements of its own cliches to describe the structure of the ideal state (Exod 19:6 *qādôš*; cf. Lev 11:44-45; Deut 7:6; 14:21; 26:18; *gôy*, cf. Deut 4:6-8, 34; II Sam 7:22-24; *mmlkh*, cf. I Kgs 18:10). This text is recapitulated in its polar opposite (Exod 24:1-12) and together they determine the meaning that is to be given to the word 'covenant' in the J Sinai covenant.

94. Num 10:33-36 is a pastiche of theological ideas and typical expressions. The journey from Sinai (10:33a[a]) was described first by P (Num 10:11-12); the three-day journey (10:33a[b]) is a standard distance (e.g. Gen 30:36; 40:12, 13, 18, 19) and is used by Dtr² in describing the exodus (Exod 3:18; 5:3; 8:23; 15:22; Num 33:8) and the crossing of the Jordan (Josh 1:11; 3:2); the idea of reconnoitering the land (10:33b[b]) is taken from the J and P spy narrative (Num 13-14); the ark of the covenant is a Dtr² idea (e.g. Deut 10:1-9); the notion of rest (10:33b[b] *mĕnûḥâ*) is familiar to Dtr² (Deut 3:20; 12:9; Josh 23:1; II Sam 7:1, 11; I Kgs 8:56); the cloud (10:34a) belongs in the J (Exod 34:5) and P narratives (Exod 24:15-18); the camp is known to P (e.g. Exod 16:13) and E (e.g. Gen 32:9; 33:8; Exod 32:19) and is a favorite locus of Dtr² (e.g. Gen 50:9; Exod 19:17; Num 5:2; 11:1, 9, 30, 31, 32; 14:44; Deut 23:11-12; Josh 1:11; 3:2; 6:11, 14: 8:13; 9:6, 10:6, 15, 21, 43; I Sam 4:3, 5, 6, 7); the address to the ark (10:35-36) combines topics congenial to Dtr² such as travel (*nsᶜ*) and rest (*nwḥ*), flight (*nws*) and defeat of the enemy (*᾽yb / śn᾽*); cf. N. Lohfink, "Die Schichten des Pentateuch und der Krieg," N. Lohfink, ed., *Gewalt und Gewaltlosigkeit im Alten Testament*, Freiburg: Herder, 1983, 51-110.

95. Noth, *ÜS*, 5-6. Among the speeches Noth includes Josh 1 and 23, I Sam 12, I Kgs 8:14ff; among the summaries, Josh 12, Judg 2:11ff, II Kgs 17:7ff. These texts (cf. also Josh 24; Judg 6:1-10; 10:6-16; I Sam 8) introduce and explain Dtr²'s own material and are filled with its cliches.

96. S.J. de Vries, "The Origin of the Murmuring Tradition," *JBL* 87 (1968) 51-58; P. Buis, "Les conflits entre Moïse et Israël dans Exode et Nombres," *VT* 28 (1978) 257-270; D. Jobling, *The Sense of Biblical Narrative: Three Structural Analyses in the Old Testament (I Samuel 13-31; Numbers 11-12; I Kings 17-18)*, Sheffield: The University of Sheffield, 1978; H. Seebass, "Num XI, XII und die Hypothese des Jahwisten," *VTS* 28 (1978) 214-223; H. Reviv, "The Traditions Concerning the Inception of the Legal System in Israel: Significance and Dating," *ZAW* 94 (1982) 566-575.

97. Judg 6:7-10; 10:10-16; and the "framework" texts: cf. W. Richter, *Die Bearbeitung des 'Retterbuches' in der deuteronomischen Epoche* [BBB, 21],Bonn: Peter Hanstein, 1964.

98. The most obvious example is the defeat of Sihon and Og that Dtr^2 considers the model of the conquest and settlement: Num 21:21-35; Deut 2:26-3:11; 3:18-22; 29:6-7; 31:4; Josh 2:10; 9:10; 12:1-6; 13:8-33; Judg 11:18-23.

99. Martin Noth, *Numbers. A Commentary*, trans., J.D. Martin, Philadelphia: Westminster, 1968, 194-198; G. E. Mendenhall, "The Incident at Beth Baal Peor," *The Tenth Generation. The Origins of the Biblical Tradition*, Baltimore: Johns Hopkins University, 1973, 105-121. Similarly, Moses is the model of prophecy (Deut 18:15), Samuel is the perfect judge (I Sam 12:1-5), David is the model king and Jeroboam represents everything that was wrong with the monarchy (I Kgs 2:1-4; II Kgs 17:21-22), Josiah is the example of repentance (II Kgs 23:25), etc.

100. B. Peckham, "The Composition of Joshua 3-4," *CBQ* 46 (1984) 413-431.

101. T. Veijola, *Die Ewige Dynastie. David und die Entstehung seiner Dynastie nach der deuteronomistischen Darstellung*, Helsinki, 1975.

102. B. Peckham, "The Composition of Joshua 3-4," *CBQ* 46 (1984) 413-431; "The Deuteronomistic History of Saul and David," *ZAW* 97 (1985) [forthcoming].

103. Noth (*ÜS*, 4-5) considered that Dtr language was simple, artless and inelegant, noted that it was characterized by regular recurrence and slight variation, and assumed that it was too well known to require analysis. But although he made language the only criterion for distinguishing Dtr from its sources, he continued to identify Dtr by its special interests, to confine it to critical comments, and to limit its language to cliches and mannerisms.

104. In the E story Joseph hears that his father is ill and goes to visit him (Gen 48:1-2), but Dtr^2 announces the imminent death of Israel and has him summon Joseph to his sick bed (Gen 47:29, 31b; 49:33a). According to E Joseph swore to bury Jacob in the tomb he had dug in Canaan (Gen 48:21; 50:5), but Dtr^2 interprets this as burial with his fathers in the plot

Abraham had purchased (Gen 47:29b-31a; 49:29-32). E portrays the adoption of Ephraim and Manasseh as a blessing for the future (Gen 48:8-21), but Dtr[2] includes it in an historical retrospect (Gen 48:3-7). E describes a period of mourning in Egypt before the journey to Canaan (Gen 50:1-8, 14), but Dtr[2] situates it in Transjordan before the burial at Machphelah (Gen 50:9-13).

105. P. D. Hanson, "The Song of Heshbon and David's *NÎR*," *HTR* 61 (1968) 297-320; J. R. Bartlett, "The Historical Reference of Num 21:27-30," *PEQ* 101 (1969) 94-100; L. T. Geraty, "Heshbon: The First Casualty in the Israelite Quest of the Kingdom of God," H. B. Huffmon *et al* eds., *The Quest for the Kingdom of God: Studies in Honor of George E. Mendenhall*, Winona Lake: Eisenbrauns, 1983, 239-248.

106. N. Lohfink, "Hos 11:5 als Bezugstext von Dtn 17:16," *VT* 31 (1981) 226-228; R.E. Friedman, "From Egypt to Egypt: Dtr[1] and Dtr[2]," B. Halpern - J. D. Levenson, eds., *Traditions in Transformation. Turning Points in Biblical Faith*, Winona Lake: Eisenbrauns, 1981, 167-192.

107. Gen 6:4; Num 13:33; Deut 2:10-12, 20-23; 3:11, 13.

108. Gen 11:9a; 21:27b-31; 22:14; 26:18-22, 32-33; 50:11; Exod 15:23; 17:7; I Sam 7:7.

109. Gen 3:20; 4:1; 16:11; 29:31-30:24.

110. Gen 3:7b, 21; 4:2; 9:20; 10:9.

111. Gen 32:26, 32b-33; Exod 12:24-27; Deut 6:20-25; Josh 4:20-24; 9:22-27; I Sam 5:5.

112. Num 13:16b; Deut 3:9; 34:1; Josh 15:8-10; Judg 1:10, 23.

113. Exod 16:36; Num 11:7-9; I Sam 9:9.

114. Gen 34:13; 35:22, 26; 46:26; I Kgs 18:31; II Kgs 17:34.

115. Gen 46:8; Exod 3:15; Lev 11:2; Num 1:2; Deut 1:3; Josh 1:2; Judg 2:11; I Sam 10:18; II Sam 7:6; I Kgs 8:1; II Kgs 17:7.

116. Dtr[2]'s ideas on primitive tribal organization may have been influenced by the contemporary Greek amphictyonies: cp. H. Bengston, *Die Verträge der griechisch-römischen Welt von 700 bis 338v. Chr.* [*Die Staatsverträge des Altertums, II*], Munich: C. H. Beck 1962; H. E. Chambers, "Ancient Amphictyonies, Sic et Non," W. W. Hallo *et al* eds., *Scripture in Context, II: More Essays on the Comparative Method*, Winona Lake: Eisenbrauns, 1983, 39-59.

117. Gen 29:24, 29, 31-35; 30:1-24.

118. Gen 35:16-26; 44:18-34; 46:8-27; 48:3-7.

119. Gen 49:1-28; Deut 33.

120. Num 1-2; 10:13-36; 13:4-16; 26; 31.

121. Josh 13-21; Judg 1.

122. Num 27:11; 32:1-42; 36:1-12; Deut 3:12-17; 4:41-43; Josh 1:12-18; 4:12-13; 13:8-31; 22:1-34.

123. Exod 6:14-25; 32:26-29; Num 3-4, 7-8; Deut 10:8-9; Josh 21; Judg 19-21; I Sam 6:15; II Sam 15:24; I Kgs 8:4; 12:31 etc.

124. I Sam 11:8; 17:1a[b]b, 52-54; 18:16; II Sam 2:4, 10; 5:3; 11:11, 20:1-2; I Kgs 1:35; 11:27-39; 12:16-20; 13:1-32; II Kgs 17:19-21; cf. R. Smend, "Gehörte Juda zum vorstaatlichen Israel?," *Fourth World Congress of Jewish Studies. Papers, I*, Jerusalem, 1967, 57-62; S. Herrmann, "Autonome Entwicklungen in den Königreichen Israel und Juda," *VTS* 17 (1969) 139-158; R. de Vaux, "The Settlement of the Israelites in Southern Palestine and the Origins of the Tribe of Judah," H. T. Frank - W. L. Reed, eds., *Translating and Understanding the Old Testament*, Nashville: Abingdon, 1970, 108-134.

125. Num 1-10; 13:4-16; Deut 1:9-18; 5:23; 29:9b-10.

126. Exod 3:16; 4:29; 12:21; 24:1-11; Num 11:16; 22:7; Deut 5:23; 21:1-9; 22:13-21; 27:1; 29:9b; 31:9, 28; Josh 23:1; 24:1; Judg 2:7.

127. I Sam 9:21; 10:17-27a; II Sam 3:17-21; 5:3; I Kgs 11:27-39.

128. Deut 12:10; 25:19; Josh 21:44; 23:1; Judg 8:34; I Sam 12:11; 14:47; II Sam 7:1; cp. I Kgs 5:4, 18.

129. Gen 15:16; Josh 13:1-7; 24:11; Judg 1: I Kgs 9:20-21; II Kgs 21:11.

130. Exod 17:8-16; Num 24:20; Deut 25:17-19; I Sam 15 mention Amalek; Judg 13-16; I Sam 4-6; II Sam 5:17-25; 19:10 deal with the Philistines.

131. Num 22:4, 7; 25:16-18: 31:1-12; Judg 6-8.

132. Num 24:18; I Sam 14:47; II Sam 8:14; I Kgs 11:14-22; II Kgs 14:7.

133. Exod 6-12; 15:22-26; Deut 17:16; 28:27, 60; II Kgs 18-21, 23-24.

134. Deut 4:25-31; 28:36-37, 47-57; Judg 3:7-11; II Kgs 23:26-27.

135. II Sam 5:11-12; 8:9-12; I Kgs 5:15-32; 9:10-14, 26-28; 10: 1-22.

136. Josh 8:29, 30-35; 10:27; Judg 6:25, 28; II Kgs 14: 6; 23:21-23.

137. Gen 15:6; 18:19; 20:12-13; 22:15-18; 26:2-5, 23-25.

138. Josh 11:15; I Kgs 15:5; II Kgs 18:6; 23:25.

139. Gen 16:13-14; Exod 3:5; Josh 5:15.

140. Gen 8:21; 12:7, 8b; 26:25; 33:20; Exod 20:24-26; 24:4; 27:1-8; Deut 27:1-8; Josh 8:30-35; 22:10.

141. Gen 31:49; 32:30; Josh 5:10; 18:1; I Sam 7:5; 10:8; II Sam 24:18; I Kgs 3:4.

142. Gen 31:19, 30-35; Num 21:4-9.

143. Gen 35:14; Exod 3:18; 24:1-11; Judg 6:19-24; I Sam 2:12-17; 7:9; 9:12, 24; 13:8-15; 15:22; II Sam 6:13; I Kgs 8:62-64.

144. Num 21:29; Deut 7:5; 16:21; Judg 2:13; 6:25, 28; 9:4, 46; I Sam 5:1-5; I Kgs 11:1-8; 16:31-33; II Kgs 1:2; 17:29-34; 23:13-14.

145. Gen 14:18-20; 21:33; 24:3; 33:20; 48:3; I Sam 4:4; cf. F. M. Cross, *Canaanite Myth and Hebrew Epic*, 1-75; J. Van Seters, "The Religion of the Patriarchs in Genesis," *Bib* 61 (1980) 220-233.

146. Exod 25-31; 33:7-11; 35-40.

147. I Kgs 6-9; II Kgs 12:5-17; 16:10-18; 18:16; 22:3-7; 25:8-17.

148. Exod 29; Lev 8-10.

149. Num 3-4, 7-8, 16-18.

150. Num 5-6, 19, 30; Deut 26:1-15; 31:9-13.

151. Num 1:1; 9:1; Deut 1:3; 2:14; Josh 5:6.

152. Exod 12:14-20; Num 28-29; Deut 14-16; Josh 3-5; I Kgs 12:32.

153. Exod 16:4-5, 8, 16-34, 35b, 36; 20:8-11; 31:12-17; 34:21; 35:1-3; Num 15:32-36; 28:9-10; Deut 5:12-15; II Kgs 11:4-12; 16:18.

154. Exod 12:14-20; 13:3-10; 34:18; Deut 16:1-8; Judg 6: 19-24.

155. Exod 4:21-23; 11:4-8; 12:29-32; 13:1-2, 11-16; Num 3:11-13, 40-51; 8:14-19; Josh 6:26; I Kgs 16:34.

156. Exod 3:18; 5:3; 8:23; 9:5, 18; 10:22-23; 15:22; Num 24:14; Josh 1:11; 3:2; 9:16; Judg 19:4; II Sam 20:4; I Kgs 12:5.

157. Gen 8:22; 29:14; Exod 9:31-32; 34:21; Judg 21:19-21.

158. Gen 15:12, 17; 19:1, 15, 23; 24:11; Exod 11:4; 12:29; 16:8, 21; Num 22:19-21; Josh 10:12-14, 27; I Sam 9:19, 26; 14:24.

159. II Kgs 17:1-6; 20:1-7; II Kgs 25:1-21.

160. Deut 1:9-18; 16:18-17:13; 19:15-21; 25:1-3.

161. II Sam 14; 15:4-6; I Kgs 3:16-28.

162. Gen 16:5; 18:22-33; 31:53; Exod 22:9-12; I Kgs 8:31-32; cf. P. K. McCarter, "The River Ordeal in Israelite Literature," *HTR* 66 (1973) 403-412.

163. II Kgs 17:7-23; 22:13; 23:26-27.

164. I Kgs 14:4-16; II Kgs 8:7-15; 9:1-10.

165. Gen 15; 18:17-19; 20:7; II Kgs 17:13-18; 22:14-20.

166. Exod 14:11-14; 15:1-21; 17:8-16; Num 14:42; 21:1-3; Deut 1:30; 3:22; 31:4; Josh 5:13-15; 10:14, 42; Judg 5:20, 23.

167. Num 21:1-3; Deut 7:2; 20:1-20; Josh 7.

168. *nāgîd*, I Sam 9:16; 10:1; 13:14; 25:30; II Sam 5:2; 6:21; 7:8; I Kgs 1:35; 14:7; 16:2; II Kgs 20:5. The term is applied to David and his line as *māšîaḥ*, "anointed" is reserved for Saul and the kings of Israel (I Sam 2:10, 35; 12:3, 5; 16:6; 24:7; 26:9, 11, 23; II Sam 1:14, 16; 19:22; 22:51; 23:1). Both terms were coined by Dtr[2] to express the theocratic ideal of government. Cf. E. Lipiński, "*nāgîd*, der Kronprinz," *VT* 24 (1974) 497-499; T. N. D. Mettinger, *King and Messiah. The Civil and Sacral Legitimation of the Israelite Kings*, Lund: C. W. K. Gleerup, 1976, 151-184.

169. Gen 21:30; 31:48, 50, 52; Josh 22:27, 28, 34; 24:27; I Sam 12:5.

170. Deut 4:26; 8:19; 30:19; 31:28; 32:46.

171. Deut 3:21; 4:3, 9; 7:19; 10:21; 11:2, 7: 29:2.

172. Deut 4:32-40; 7:6-11; 8:2-6; 9:4-6; 11:2-7; 29:1b-8; II Sam 7:18-29; cf. N. Lohfink, *Das Hauptgebot. Eine Untersuchung literarischer Einleitungsfragen zu Dtn 5-11*, Rome: Biblical Institute Press, 1963, 125-131.

173. Num 21:14; Josh 10:13; II Sam 1:18.

174. The ballad of Jael tells the story of the defeat of Sisera (Judg 5:6-7a, 8b, 10-11a, 14, 15b-17, 19, 21a, 22, 24a[a]b, 25-30). The Dtr[2] version (Judg 5:1-5, 7b-8a, 9, 11b-13, 15a, 18, 20, 21b, 23, 24a[b], 31) converts it into a model of holy war in which it is Yahweh rather than any other agent that

defeats the enemy (cf. Judg 4:23-24).

175. cf. n. 92, above.

176. Gen 8:7, 13b, 20-22; Gilgamesh XI, 135, 152-169.

177. Exod 3:7b; 15:26; Jer 30:12-15; cf. N. Lohfink, "'Ich bin Jahwe, dein Arzt' (Exod 15, 26)," H. Merklein - E. Zenger, eds., *"Ich will euer Gott werden." Beispiele biblischen Redens von Gott* [SBS, 100], Stuttgart: Katholisches Bibelwerk, 1981, 11-73.

178. Gen 2:10-14; Ezek 47:1-12; cf. J. D. Levenson, *Theology of the Program of Restoration of Ezekiel 40-48*, Missoula: Scholars, 1976, 7-19.

179. Gen 3:24; Ezek 28:16.

180. Exod 31:12-17; Ezek 20:10-26; cf. M. Greenberg, *Ezekiel 1-20* [AB, 22], Garden City: Doubleday, 1983, 360-388.

181. Exod 19:5; 34:28; Deut 4:13.

182. Exod 24:7; Deut 29:20; 30:10; 31:26; II Kgs 22:8, 11; 23:2, 21.

183. *ḥrh ɔp* is a favorite Dtr[2] expression (Gen 18:30, 32; Exod 4:14; 15:7-8; Num 11:1, 10, 33; 12:9; 22:22; 25:3, 4: 32:10, 13, 14; Deut 13:18; Josh 7:1, 26; Judg 2:14, 20; 3:8; 10:7; II Sam 6:7; 24:1; II Kgs 13:3). It was used first by E (Gen 39:19; Exod 22:23; 32:19, 22) and then by Habakkuk (Hab 3:8); cf. D. J. McCarthy, "The Wrath of Yahweh and the Structural Unity of the Deuteronomistic History," J. L. Crenshaw and J. T. Willis, eds., *Essays in Old Testament Ethics. J. Philip Hyatt in Memoriam*, New York: Ktav, 1974, 99-110.

184. Deut 6:15; 7:4; 11:17; 29:26; 31:17; Josh 23:16; II Kgs 17:18; 23:26; cf. N. Lohfink, "Kerygmata des deuteronomistischen Geschichtswerks," J. Jeremias - L. Perlitt, eds., *Die Botschaft und die Boten. Festschrift für H. W. Wolff zum 70. Geburtstag*, Neukirchen-Vluyn: Neukirchener Verlag, 1981, 87-100.

185. Exod 7:17; 8:6, 18-19; 9:16; 10:1-2; Deut 7:18-19.

186. Exod 8:19; 9:4, 26; 10:23; 11:7.

187. Gen 14:19; 24:3, 7; Exod 20:22; 24:10; Deut 4:36; I Kgs 8:27-30.

188. Exod 8:4-9a, 24-25; 9:27-35; Deut 4:7; I Kgs 8:31-53.

189. Gen 33:20; Exod 24:10; 34:23; Num 16:9; Josh 7:3, 19, 20; 8:30; 9:18, 19. The epithet was coined by Dtr[2] from the E designation "God of your fathers ...." (Gen 31:42; 46:3; 50:17; Exod 3:6, 13).

190. Lev 7:37-38; 11:46-47; 16:29-34; 27:34.

191. Lev 3:17; 5:20-26; 7:37-38; 12:7-8; 13:59; 14:54-57; 15:32-33; 16:29-34; 18:24-30; 20:22-27; 22:31-33; 24:10-23; 26:46; 27:34.

192. Cf. D. W. Baker, "Division Markers and the Structure of Leviticus 1-7," *Studia Biblica, I* [JSOTSS, 11], Sheffield: University of Sheffield, 1978, 9-15; A. Cholewiński, *Heiligkeitsgesetz und Deuteronomium. Eine vergleichende Studie* [AnBib, 66], Rome: Biblical Institute Press, 1976; M. Fishbane, "Revelation and Tradition: Aspects of Inner-Biblical Exegesis," *JBL* 99 (1980) 343-361; "Biblical Colophons, Textual Criticism and Legal Analogies," *CBQ* 42 (1980) 438-449; M. Haran, *Temples and Temple-Service in Ancient Israel. An Inquiry into the Character of Cult Phenomena and the Historical Setting of the Priestly School*, Oxford: Clarendon, 1978; A. Hurvitz, *A Linguistic Study of the Relationship between the Priestly Source and the Book of Ezekiel. A New Approach to an Old Problem*, Paris: Gabalda, 1982; B. Levine, "The Descriptive Tabernacle Texts of the Pentateuch," *JAOS* 85 (1965) 307-318; *In the Presence of the Lord. A Study of Cult and Some Cultic Terms in Ancient Israel*, Leiden: Brill, 1974; N. Lohfink, "Die Abänderung der Theologie des priesterlichen Geschichtswerks im Segen des Heiligkeitsgesetzes. Zu Lev 26, 9. 11-13," H. Gese and H. P. Rüger, eds., *Wort und Geschichte. Festschrift für Karl Elliger zum 70. Geburtstag* [AOAT, 18], Neukirchen-Vluyn: Neukirchener Verlag, 1973, 129-136; W. L. Moran, "The Literary Connection between Lv 11,13-19 and Dt 14,12-18," *CBQ* 28 (1966) 271-277; M. Noth, *Leviticus. A Commentary*. J. E. Anderson, trans., London: SCM, 1965.

193. The Chr history interprets and corrects Dtr^2 and, as in its evaluation of Hezekiah, returns to the Dtr^1 point of view: cf. P. R. Ackroyd, "The Chronicler as Exegete," *JSOT* 2 (1977) 2-32; F. M. Cross, "A Reconstruction of the Judaean Restoration," *JBL* 94 (1975) 4-18; B. Halpern, "Sacred History and Ideology: Chronicles' Thematic Structure - Indications of an Earlier Source," R. E. Friedman, ed., *The Creation of Sacred Literature. Composition and Redaction of the Biblical Text*, Berkeley: University of California, 1981, 35-54; M. Noth, *ÜS*, 110-180; T. Willi, *Die Chronik als Auslegung. Untersuchungen zur literarischen Gestaltung der historischen Überlieferung Israels* [FRLANT, 106], Göttingen: Vandenhoeck & Ruprecht, 1972.

FIGURES

Episode	Paragraph	Fig 1 - The J Narrative	Opening Markers			Closing Markers	
			wyhy	disj	cons	disj	cons
		GENESIS					
I	1	2:4b-7a, 8-9, 16-17		4b		17	
	2	2:18-19a^{a}, 20b-22, 25			18	25	
	3	3:1-7a, 8-13, 22-23		1			23
II	1	6:1-2, 4a^{b}b	1			4b	
	2	6:5-6, 7a^{a}b, 8			5	8	
	3	7:1a, 4, 7			1a		7
	4	7:10, 16b, 17, 23a^{a}*b	10				23b
	5	8:6, 8-12	6			12b	
III	1	11:1-3	1			3	
	2	11:4-7, 8b, 9b			4	9b	
	3	12:1, 4a, 6a, 8a			1		8a
	4	13:2, 5, 7a, 8-9a^{a}b, 10a, 11a		2			11a
	5	13:12, 18a		12			18a
	6	18:1b, 2ab^{a}, 3-6		1b			6
	7	18:7-10		7		10	
	8	18:11-16		11		16	
	9	19:1a^{b}b^{a}, 2-3		1a^{b}			3
	10	19:4-6		4		6	
	11	19:7-8, 9a^{a}*b, 10			7	10	
	12	19:12, 13a, 14			12		14
	13	19:24a, 25, 27a, 28		24a			28
	14	21:1a, 2a, 3		1a			3
IV	1	26:1a^{a}b, 6, 7	1			7	
	2	26:8-9, 11	8			11	
	3	26:12-14, 16-17			12		17
	4	26:26-31		26			31
	5	27:1-4	1			4	
	6	27:5-16		5		16	
	7	27:17-23			17	23	
	8	27:24-29			24	29	
	9	27:30-33	30			33	
	10	27:34-35, 36b-40		34		40	
	11	27:41-44, 45b			41	45b	
	12	29:1-3			1	3	
	13	29:4-9			4	9	
	14	29:10-13a, 15	10				15

Epi-sode	Para-graph	Fig 1 - The J Narrative	Opening Markers			Closing Markers	
			wyhy	disj	cons	disj	cons
		GENESIS					
	15	29:16-22		16			22
	16	29:23, 25-28, 30	23				30
	17	30:25-36	25			36	
	18	30:37-42			37	42	
	19	32:4-7			4	7	
	20	32:14a, 25b, 27-29			14a	29	
	21	33:1a, 4, 12-16, 18a[a]			1a		18a[a]
V	1	37:3a, 4		3a		4	
	2	37:12-13, 14ab[b], 15-18			12	18	
	3	37:25-27, 28a[b]			25		28a[b]
	4	39:1, 4a, 6a		1		6a	
	5	41:54[b]; 42:1-4	54b			4	
	6	42:7-8			7	8	
	7	42:9b-13			9b	13	
	8	42:14-18a, 19-20a			14	20a	
	9	42:20b, 24, 26, 29-32			20b	32	
	10	42:33-34, 36, 38			33	38	
	11	43:1-10		1		10	
	12	43:11, 13, 14b			11	14b	
	13	43:15a[a]b, 16, 17, 23b, 24b, 25			15	25	
	14	43:26-29a, 30-32a, 33-34			26		34
	15	45:1-3		1		3	
	16	45:24-26a[a]b, 27a[a]b, 28			24		28
	17	46:28-34a		28		34a	
	18	47:1-6			1	6	
		EXODUS					
VI	1	1:8-11a, 12a, 22			8	22	
	2	2:1-3, 5-6ab[a], 10a[b]b[a]			1		10
	3	2:11-12, 15	11				15
	4	2:16-21		16			21
	5	2:23a[a]; 3:2-4a, 7a, 8; 4:19a[b]b-20a	23				20
	6	4:24-26	24			26	
	7	12:37a, 38			37a	38	
	8	13:20-22			20	22	
	9	14:5a, 6, 9a[a], 19b-20			5a	20	

Epi-sode	Para-graph	Fig 1 - The J Narrative	Opening Markers			Closing Markers	
			wyhy	disj	cons	disj	cons
		EXODUS					
	10	14:24, 27b, 30	24				30
	11	19:1b, 2b, 10a, 11, 14b[a], 15a		1b			15a
	12	19:16a[a], 18ab[a], 20; 34:5-7	16			7	
	13	34:10-12a, 14			10	14	
	14	34:19, 20b, 22, 24		19		24	
		NUMBERS					
	15	Exod 34:27; Num 13:2a[a], 17-20			27	20	
	16	13:22a, 23, 25a, 27-28			22a	28	
	17	13:30-31			30	31	
	18	14:11a, 12-19a, 20-21, 23-24			11a	24	
	19	16:12-14, 25a			12		25
	20	16:27b-32a, 33a, 34		27b		34	
	21	20:14-18			14	18	
	22	21:21-22			21		22
	23	21:23-24		23			24
	24	22:2, 5-6, 36a, 40ab[a]			2		40
	25	22:41; 23:1-4, 5b, 6a, 7-9	41			9	
	26	23:11-16a[a]b, 17-20, 22-24			11	24	
	27	23:25-30; 24:1-3a, 5-6, 8a, 9			25	9	
	28	24:10b, 11a, 25			10b	25	

Epi-sode	Para-graph	Fig 2 - The Dtr^{1} History	Opening Markers			Closing Markers	
			wyhy	disj	cons	disj	cons
		DEUTERONOMY					
I	1	1:1a; 5:1a^{a}*, 2-3		1a		3	
	2	5:4, 5*, 6-7, 9b-11		4		11	
	3	5:24a, 25, 27			24a	27	
	4	6:4-9		4			9
	5	7:1-2ab^{b}		1		2b	
	6	7:17, 21, 23, 24		17		24	
	7	10:12, 14, 17, 18, 20		12		20	
	8	11:22-25a			22	25a	
	9	12:13-14		13		14	
	10	12:20, 26		20		26	
	11	14:4-5, 11-12, 13*, 16*, 17*, 18b-20		4		20	
	12	14:22, 25-26		22			26
	13	15:19-20		19		20	
	14	16:2a, 7a, 16a^{a}b			2a	16b	
	15	29:1a, 9a, 11, 13-14			1a	14	
	16	31:1, 2a, 3a, 6			1	6	
		JOSHUA					
II	1	1:1-5ab^{b}	1			5b^{b}	
	2	2:1-7			1	7	
	3	2:8-9a, 12ab^{a}, 13-14		8		14	
	4	2:15-16, 22			15	22	
	5	2:23-24a			23	24a	
	6	3:5, 10b, 16b			5	16b	
	7	6:2, 16b, 20a^{a}b^{b}			2	20b	
	8	6:22, 23a^{a}, 25a^{a}b		22		25b	
	9	8:1-2a^{a}b, 3ab^{a}, 4-5a, 6a^{a}b, 7			1	7	
	10	8:9a^{a}, 11a, 16, 18-19a			9a^{a}		19a
	11	9:3-5		3		5	
	12	9:8-9a^{a}, 12-13, 15a^{a}			8		15a
	13	10:1a^{a}*b^{a}, 2-4a, 5, 8-9a, 10a	1a				10a
	14	11:1, 5, 6a, 7a, 8a^{a}*	1				8a^{a}
	15	11:18, 23a^{a}b		18		23b	
		I SAMUEL					
III	1	1:1-3a	1			3a	
	2	1:4-7a	4			7a	

Epi-sode	Para-graph	Fig 2 - The Dtr[1] History	Opening Markers			Closing Markers	
			wyhy	disj	cons	disj	cons
		I SAMUEL					
	3	1:7b-9a[a], 11ab[a], 18b, 19a[b]b			7b		19b
	4	1:20ab[a], 21, 22ab[a], 23a[a]b, 24a[b]	20a				24a
IV	1	9:1-2a[a]	1			2a[a]	
	2	9:3-4			3	4	
	3	9:5-6a[a]b, 10		5			10
	4	9:14b[a], 18, 19a[a], 20a		14b		20a	
	5	9:22a, 24b, 26b, 10:10a[a]			22a		10a
	6	10:27b; 11:1-2a, 4a[a], 9-10	27b				10
	7	11:11a, 14a, 15a[a]	11a				15a
	8	14:52	52a			52b	
V	1	17:1a[a], 2-3			1a[a]	3	
	2	17:4a[a], 7b-9			4a[a]		9
	3	17:12a[a], 13a, 17, 18b[a]		12a[a]		18b[a]	
	4	17:19, 21, 22a[b]b		19			22b
	5	17:23*, 25a[a]b		23		25b	
	6	17:26a[a], 27			26a	27	
	7	17:31, 32a[a]b, 40a			31	40a	
	8	17:40b, 41, 49			40b		49
	9	17:57a[a], 58; 18:2		57a		2	
	10	18:5a[b]b[a], 20, 27b			5a		27b
	11	31:1a, 2-3, 4b-6; II Sam 5:1a, 3b		1a			3b
		II SAMUEL					
VI	1	7:4b-5a, 12, 14a, 15a, 16a, 17a[a]b	4b			17b	
	2	11:1	1a			1b	
	3	11:2-3	2			3	
	4	11:14-15	14				15
	5	11:16-19, 21b-24	16			24b	
	6	11:26-27a[a]; 12:24b[a]			26		24b[a]
VII	1	13:1-2a[a]b	1				2b
	2	13:3a, 4-5		3a		5	
	3	13:6-8a			6	8a	
	4	13:8b-11, 12a[a], 14a			8b	14a	
	5	13:14b-15, 19a[a]b			14b	19b	
	6	13:23-29	23				29

Episode	Paragraph	Fig 2 - The Dtr^{1} History	Opening Markers			Closing Markers	
			wyhy	disj	cons	disj	cons
		II SAMUEL					
	7	13:30ab^{a}, 32-33	30a			33	
	8	13:34-36			34	36	
	9	15:1-3	1			3	
	10	15:7b, 9-10			7b	10	
	11	15:13, 17a, 18a			13	18a	
	12	18:1, 2b-4			1	4	
	13	18:9, 10a, 14b-15			9		15
	14	18:19-23		19			23
	15	18:24-30		24			30
	16	18:31-32; 19:1-5		31		5	
	17	19:6ab^{a}, 7-9ab^{a}			6a		9b
		I KINGS					
VIII	1	1:5, 9a^{a}b^{a}, 10		1		10	
	2	1:32-34, 38, 39a^{b}b, 40			32	40	
	3	1:41a, 49; 2:10-11, 46b			41a	46b	
	4	11:26, 40		26			40
	5	11:42-43; 12:1, 3b-4		42		4	
	6	12:6-11			6	11	
	7	12:13-15a			13	15a	
	8	12:20a, 26, 27a, 28a, 29	20a			29	
	9	14:21a, 25, 26a^{a}, 30-31		21a			31
	10	15:2, 7b-8		2			8
	11	15:10, 16-20, 24		10			24
	12	22:42, 45, 51		42			51
		II KINGS					
	13	8:17, 24		17			24
	14	8:26, 28-29		26		29	
	15	9:14a, 16a^{a}, 17-18	14a			18	
	16	9:19-20			19	20	
	17	9:21ab^{a}, 22ab^{a}, 23-24			21a		24
	18	9:27-28		27			28
	19	11:1-2a, 3		1		3	
	20	11:4ab^{b}, 12a^{b}b, 13, 16a^{a}b		4a			16b
	21	12:1, 2a^{b}b, 18-19, 21ab^{a}, 22a^{b}b		1			22b
	22	14:2, 5, 19-21		2			21
	23	15:2, 5, 7		2			7

Episode	Paragraph	Fig 2 - The Dtr^{1} History	Opening Markers			Closing Markers	
			wyhy	disj	cons	disj	cons
		II KINGS					
	24	15:33, 38		33			38
	25	16:2a, 5, 7-9a, 20		2a			20
	26	18:2, 7b		2		7b	
	27	18:$9a^{a}b$, $10a^{b}b^{b}$, 11a, $12a^{a}b$	$9a^{a}$			12b	
	28	18:13, $17ab^{a}$, 18-25		13		25	
	29	18:26-$27ab^{a}$, 28-30			26	30	
	30	18:36a; 19:8-9a, $36a^{b}b$, 37			8		37

Chap -ter	Para- graph	Fig 3 - The Priestly Document	Opening Markers			Closing Markers	
			wyhy	disj	cons	disj	cons
		GENESIS					
I	1	1:1-5a		1		5a	
	2	1:5b-8a	5b				8a
	3	1:8b-10a	8b			10a	
	4	1:10b-12			10b		12
	5	1:13-18	13				18
	6	1:19-22	19			22	
	7	1:23-27	23			27	
	8	1:28-31a			28		31a
	9	1:31b-2:4a	31b			4a	
II	1	5:1-29ab[a], 30-32		1			32
	2	6:9-13		9		13	
	3	6:14-16		14		16	
	4	6:17-22		17		22	
	5	7:6, 11, 13-16a		6		16a	
	6	7:18-20a			18	20a	
	7	7:20b-21, 24; 8:1-5			20b	5	
	8	8:13a, 14-19	13a			19	
	9	9:1, 9-11			1	11	
	10	9:12-16			12	16	
	11	9:17, 28-29			17		29
III	1	10:1-5		1		5	
	2	10:6-7, 20		6		20	
	3	10:22-23, 31-32		22		32	
	4	11:10-11		10			11
	5	11:12-13		12			13
	6	11:14-26		14			26
	7	11:27-28, 31-32		27			32
	8	12:4b-5		4b			5
	9	16:1, 3, 15-16		1		16	
	10	17:1-9	1			9	
	11	17:10-14		10		14	
	12	17:15-16			15	16	
	13	17:17-21			17	21	
	14	17:22-27			22	27	
	15	21:1b, 2b, 4-5			1b	5	
	16	23:1-6			1	6	

Chap -ter	Para- graph	Fig 3 - The Priestly Document	Opening Markers			Closing Markers	
			wyhy	disj	cons	disj	cons
		GENESIS					
	17	23:7-9			7	9	
	18	23:10-11		10		11	
	19	23:12-15			12	15	
	20	23:16-18			16		18
	21	23:19-20		19			20
	22	25:7-10		7		10	
IV	1	25:12-17		12			17
	2	25:19-26		19		26	
	3	25:27, 29-30a, 31-34			27	34	
	4	28:1-5; 35:9-12			1	12	
	5	35:13, 15, 27-29			13		29
	6	36:1-8a; 37:1, 2a[a]*		1		2a[a]	
	7	46:6-7			6	7	
	8	47:27-28; 49:33b			27		33b
		EXODUS					
V	1	1:1-4, 5b		1		5b	
	2	1:7, 12b-14		7		14	
	3	2:23a[b]b-25; 6:2-9			23a	9	
	4	6:10-12; 7:1-7			10	7	
	5	7:8-13			8	13	
	6	7:19-20, 21b-22			19	22	
	7	8:1-3, 9b-11			1	11	
	8	8:12-15			12	15	
	9	9:8-12			8	12	
	10	11:9-10			9	10	
	11	12:1-5			1	5	
	12	12:6, 8-10		6		10	
	13	12:11, 28		11		28	
	14	12:40-42		40		42	
	15	14:1-2			1	2	
	16	14:3-4, 8a, 9a[b]b, 10b[b], 15-18, 21-22		3		22	
	17	14:23, 26, 27a, 28a, 29			23	29	
	18	15:27; 16:1-3, 6-7			27	7	
	19	16:9-15, 35a			9	35a	
	20	17:1ab[a]; 19:1a, 2a; 24:15-17			1a	17	

Chap -ter	Para- graph	Fig 3 - The Priestly Document	Opening Markers			Closing Markers	
			wyhy	disj	cons	disj	cons
		EXODUS					
	21	24:18; 25:1-5, 8, 9a[a]b			18	9b	
	22	26:1-5		1		5	
	23	26:6-13			6	13	
	24	26:14-25			14	25	
	25	26:26-30; 29:43, 45-46			26	46	
	26	35:1a, 4b-7, 10			1a	10	
	27	35:20, 22-26, 29			20	29	
	28	36:2-7			2	7	
	29	36:8-12			8	12	
	30	36:13-22			13	22	
	31	36:23-30			23	30	
	32	36:31-38; 40:16			31	16	
	33	40:17-19, 35b-37	17			37	
		NUMBERS					
	34	10:11-12; 12:16b; 13:1, 3	11			3	
	35	13:21, 26a, 32, 33b			21	33b	
	36	14:1a, 2-4			1a	4	
	37	14:26-29, 30-32, 35-38			26	38	
	38	20:1a[b], 2-5			1a[b]	5	
	39	20:7-13			7	13	
	40	20:22-25, 27, 28a[b]b, 29; 22:1			22		1
	41	27:12-13, 15-21			12		21
		DEUTERONOMY					
	42	Num 27:22-23; Deut 32:48-50, 52			22	52	
	43	34:1a[ag]b, 2-5, 7-9			1a	9	

Part	Para-graph	Fig 4 - The Elohist Version	Opening Markers			Closing Markers	
			wyhy	disj	cons	disj	cons
		GENESIS					
I	1	20:1a[a]b, 2-3			1	3	
	2	20:8, 10-11			8	11	
	3	20:14-15			14		15
	4	20:16; 21:6-7		16		7	
	5	21:8-10, 14-16a			8	16a	
	6	21:16b, 19-20			16b		20
	7	21:22-24	22				24
	8	21:25-27a, 32, 34		25			34
	9	22:1-3	1				3
	10	22:4-8a		4		8a	
	11	22:8b-10, 13, 19			8b		19
II	1	28:10-12			10	12	
	2	28:17-19			17	19	
	3	28:20, 21a, 22			20	22	
	4	29:13b-14; 30:43; 31:1-2			13	2	
	5	31:4-5			4	5	
	6	31:6-9		6			9
	7	31:10-13	10			13	
	8	31:14-18			14		18
	9	31:19a, 20-25		19a		25	
	10	31:26-29			26	29	
	11	31:36b, 38-42			36b	42	
	12	31:43-47, 51-54; 32:1			43		1
	13	32:2-3, 8-9		2		9	
	14	32:14b-22			14b	22	
	15	32:23b, 24b; 33:3, 5, 8-11, 17			23b	17	
	16	35:1-7			1		7
III	1	37:2a[b]b, 3b			2a[b]	3b	
	2	37:5-11			5	11	
	3	37:19-22			19	22	
	4	37:23-24	23			24	
	5	37:28a[a]b, 29-30			28	30	
	6	37:31-33			31	33	
	7	37:34-35			34		35
	8	37:36; 39:4b		36		4b	
	9	39:6b-10			6b	10	
	10	39:11-18	11				18

Part	Para-graph	Fig 4 - The Elohist Version	Opening Markers			Closing Markers	
			wyhy	disj	cons	disj	cons
		GENESIS					
	11	39:19-20	19				20
	12	40:1-8	1			8	
	13	40:9-15			9	15	
	14	40:16-23			16	23	
	15	41:1-7	1			7	
	16	41:8-13	8			13	
	17	41:14-24			14	24	
	18	41:25-28			25	28	
	19	41:29-36		29		36	
	20	41:37-40			37	40	
	21	41:41-45			41		45
	22	41:46-49		46		49	
	23	41:50-52		50		52	
	24	41:53-54a, 55-57			53	57	
	25	42:5-6, 9a, 21-23			5	23	
	26	45:4-15			4	15	
	27	45:16-23		16		23	
	28	46:1-5; 47:7-12			1		12
	29	47:13-22		13		22	
	30	47:23-26			23	26	
	31	48:1-2, 8-9	1			9	
	32	48:10-14		10		14	
	33	48:15-19			15	19	
	34	48:20-21			20	21	
	35	50:1-8			1	8	
	36	50:14-21a			14	21a	
	37	50:21b-26			21b		26
		EXODUS					
IV	1	3:1, 4b, 6a, 9-12		1		12	
	2	3:13-14; 4:18			13	18	
	3	13:17-19	17			19	
	4	14:5b, 7, 8b			5b	8b	
	5	14:10ab[a], 19a, 25a, 28b		10a		28b	
	6	18:1a, 2a, 3-5, 12			1a		12
	7	18:13-18	13			18	
	8	18:19-20		19			20

Part	Para-graph	Fig 4 - The Elohist Version	Opening Markers			Closing Markers	
			wyhy	disj	cons	disj	cons
		EXODUS					
	9	18:21-23		21		23	
	10	18:24-27			24		27
	11	19:3a, 14, 16a[b]b-17, 18b[b]-19		3a		19	
	12	20:1; 21:2-6			1	6	
	13	21:7-11		7		11	
	14	21:12-14		12		14	
	15	21:15-17		15		17	
	16	21:18-19		18		19	
	17	21:20-21		20		21	
	18	21:22-25		22		25	
	19	21:26-27		26		27	
	20	21:28-32		28		32	
	21	21:33-36		33		36	
	22	21:37; 22:1-3		37		3	
	23	22:4-8		4		8	
	24	22:20-23		20		23	
	25	22:24-26		24		26	
	26	22:27-30		27		30	
	27	23:1-3		1		3	
	28	23:4-9		4		9	
	29	23:10-13		10		13	
	30	23:14, 15a[a]*, 16		14		16	
	31	23:20-22, 25b-26		20		26	
	32	23:27-31a		27			31a
	33	24:13-14			13	14	
	34	32:1-4, 6b, 15-18			1	18	
	35	32:19-21a, 22-25	19			25	
	36	34:29b-32a, 33		29b			33

Book	Part	Chap -ter	Fig 5 - The Dtr^{2} History
I			GENESIS
	A	1	[1:1-2:4a = P]
		2	2:7b, 10-14, 15, 19a^{b}b-20a, 23-24
		3	3:7b, 14-20, 21, 24
		4	4:1-26
	B	1	5:29b^{b}
		2	6:3, 4a^{a}, 7a^{bg}
		3	7:1b-3, 5, 8, 9, 12, 22, 23a*
		4	8:7, 13b, 20-22
		5	9:2-7, 8, 18-27
	C	1	10:8-19, 21, 24-30
		2	11:8a, 9a, 29-30
		3	12:2-3, 6b, 7, 8b, 9-20
		4	13:1, 3-4, 6, 7b, 9a^{b}, 10b, 11b, 13-17, 18b
		5	14:1-24
	D	1	15:1-21
		2	16:2, 4-14
		3	[17:1-27 = P]
		4	18:1a, 2b^{b}, 17-33
		5	19:1a^{a}b^{b}, 9a*, 11, 13b, 15-23, 24b, 26, 27b, 29-38
		6	20:1a^{b}, 4-7, 9, 12-13, 17-18
		7	21:27b-31, 33
		8	22:11-12, 14-18, 20-24
		9	[23:1-20 = P]
		10	24:1-67
	E	1	25:1-6, 11, 18, 28, 30b
		2	26:1a^{b}, 2-5, 10, 15, 18-25, 32-35
		3	27:36a, 45a, 46
		4	28:6-9, 13-16, 21b
		5	29:24, 29, 31-35
		6	30:1-24
		7	31:3, 19b, 30-35, 36a, 37, 48-50
		8	32:10-13, 23a, 24a, 25a, 26, 30-33

Book	Part	Chap-ter	Fig 5 - The Dtr^2 History
			GENESIS
		9	33:1b-2, 6-7, 18a^{b}b-20
		10	34:1-31
		11	35:8, 14, 16-26
	F	1	36:8b-43
		2	37:2a^g, 14b^a
		3	38:1-30
		4	39:2-3, 5, 21-23
		5	[40:1-23 = E]
		6	[41:1-54a, 55-57 = E; 41:54b = J]
		7	42:18b, 25, 27, 28, 35, 37
		8	43:12, 14a, 15a^b, 18-23a, 24a, 29b, 32b, 34
		9	44:1-34
		10	45:26a^b, 27a^b
	G	1	46:8-27, 34b
		2	47:29-31
		3	48:3-7, 22
		4	49:1-33a
		5	50:9-13
II			EXODUS
	A	1	1:5a, 6, 11b, 15-21
		2	2:4, 6b^b-10a^{a}b^b, 13-14, 22
		3	3:5, 6b, 7b, 15-22
		4	4:1-17, 19a^a, 20b-23, 27-31
		5	5:1-23
	B	1	6:1, 13-30
		2	7:14-18, 21a, 23-29
		3	8:4-9a, 16-28
		4	9:1-7, 13-35
		5	10:1-29
		6	11:1-8
		7	12:7, 12-27, 29-36, 37b, 39, 43-51

Book	Part	Chap -ter	Fig 5 - The Dtr^2 History
			EXODUS
	C	1	13:1-16
		2	14:11-14, 25b, 31
		3	15:1-26
		4	16:4-5, 8, 16-34, 35b, 36
		5	17:1b-16
		6	18:1b, 2b, 6-11
	D	1	19:3b-9, 10b, 12-13, 14b[b], 15b, 21-25
		2	20:2-26
		3	21:1
		4	22:9-19
		5	23:15a*, 17-19, 23-25a, 31b-33
		6	24:1-12
	E	1	25:6-7, 9a[b], 10-40
		2	26:31-37
		3	27:1-21
		4	28:1-43
		5	29:1-42, 44
		6	30:1-38
		7	31:1-18
	F	1	32:5-6a, 7-14, 21b, 26-35
		2	33:1-23
		3	34:1-4, 8-9, 12b, 13, 15-18, 20a, 21, 23, 25-26, 28, 29a, 32b, 34-35
	G	1	35:1b-4a, 8-9, 11-19, 21, 27-28, 30-35
		2	36:1
		3	37:1-29
		4	38:1-31
		5	39:1-43
		6	40:1-15, 20-35a, 38

Book	Part	Chap-ter	Fig 5 - The Dtr^2 History
III			LEVITICUS
	A	1	8:1-36
		2	9:1-24
		3	10:1-20
		4	11:1-45
			NUMBERS
	B	1	1:1-54
		2	2:1-33
		3	3:1-51
		4	4:1-49
		5	5:1-31
		6	6:1-27
		7	7:1-89
		8	8:1-26
		9	9:1-23
		10	10:1-10, 13-36
	C	1	11:1-35
		2	12:1-16a
		3	13:2a[b]b, 4-16, 22b, 24, 25b, 26b, 29, 33a
		4	14:1b, 6-10, 11b, 19b, 22, 25, 33-34, 39-45
		5	15:1-41
		6	16:1-11, 15-24, 25b-27a, 32b, 33b, 35
		7	17:1-28
		8	18:1-32
		9	19:1-22
	D	1	20:1b, 6, 19-21, 28a[a]
		2	21:1-20, 25-35
		3	22:3-4, 7-35, 36b-39, 40b[b]
		4	23:5a, 6b, 10, 16a[b], 17a[b], 21
		5	24:3b-4, 7, 8b, 10a, 11-24
		6	25:1-19
	E	1	26:1-65
		2	27:1-11

Book	Part	Chap -ter	Fig 5 - The Dtr^2 History
			NUMBERS
		3	28:1-31
		4	29:1-39
		5	30:1-17
		6	31:1-54
	F	1	32:1-42
		2	33:1-56
		3	34:1-29
		4	35:1-34
		5	36:1-13
IV			DEUTERONOMY
	A	1	1:1b-46
		2	2:1-37
		3	3:1-29
	B	1	4:1-49
		2	5:1*, 5, 8-9a, 12-23, 24b, 26, 28-33
		3	6:1-3, 10-25
		4	7:2b[ag], 3-16, 18-20, 22, 25-26
		5	8:1-20
		6	9:1-29
		7	10:1-11, 13, 15-16, 19, 21-22
		8	11:1-21, 25b-32
	C	1	12:1-12, 15-19, 21-25, 27-31
		2	13:1-19
		3	14:1-3, 6-10, 13*, 16*, 17*, 18a, 23, 24, 27-29
		4	15:1-18, 21-23
		5	16:1, 2b-6, 7b-15, 16a[b], 17-22
		6	17:1-20
		7	18:1-22
	D	1	19:1-21
		2	20:1-20
		3	21:1-23

Book	Part	Chap-ter	Fig 5 - The Dtr^{2} History
			DEUTERONOMY
		4	22:1-29
		5	23:1-26
		6	24:1-22
		7	25:1-19
	E	1	26:1-19
		2	27:1-26
		3	28:1-69
		4	29:1b-8, 9b-10, 12, 15-28
		5	30:1-20
	F	1	31:2b, 3b-5, 7-30
		2	32:1-47, 51
		3	33:1-29
		4	34:1a^{b}, 6, 10-12
V			JOSHUA
	A	1	1:1b^{b}, 5b^{a}, 6-18
		2	2:9b-11, 12b^{b}, 17-21, 24b
		3	3:1-4, 6-10a, 11-16a, 17
		4	4:1-24
		5	5:1-15
		6	6:1, 3-16a, 17-19, 20a^{b}b^{a}, 21, 23a^{b}, 24, 25a^{b}, 26-27
		7	7:1-26
		8	8:2a^{b}, 3b^{b}, 5b, 6a^{b}, 8, 9a^{b}b, 10, 11b-15, 17-18, 19*, 20-35
	B	1	9:1-2, 6-7, 9a^{b}-11, 14, 15a^{b}b-27
		2	10:1a^{a}*, 4b, 6-7, 9b, 10b-43
		3	11:2-4, 6b, 8*, 9-17, 19-22, 23a^{b}
	C	1	12:1-24
		2	13:1-33
		3	14:1-15
		4	15:1-63
		5	16:1-10

Book	Part	Chap -ter	Fig 5 - The Dtr^{2} History
			DEUTERONOMY
		6	17:1-18
		7	18:1-28
		8	19:1-51
		9	20:1-9
		10	21:1-45
		11	22:1-34
		12	23:1-16
		13	24:1-33
VI			JUDGES
	A	1-5	1:1-5:31
	B	1-4	6:1-9:57
	C	1-3	10:1-12:15
	D	1-4	13:1-16:31
	E	1-5	17:1-21:25
VII			I SAMUEL
	A	1	1:3b, 9a^{b}b-10, 11b^{b}-18a, 19a^{a}, 20b^{b}, 22b^{b}, 23a^{b}, 24a^{a}b, 25-28
		2	2:1-36
		3	3:1-21
		4	4:1-22
		5	5:1-12
		6	6:1-21
		7	7:1-17
	B	1	8:1-22
		2	9:2a^{b}b, 6a^{b}, 7-9, 11-14a^{a}, 14b^{b}-17, 19a^{b}b, 20b-21, 22b-24a, 25-26a, 27
		3	10:1-9, 10a^{b}b-27a
		4	11:2b-3, 4a^{b}b-8, 11b-13, 14b, 15a^{b}b
		5	12:1-25
		6	13:1-23
		7	14:1-51
		8	15:1-35

Book	Part	Chap -ter	Fig 5 - The Dtr^{2} History
			I SAMUEL
	C	1	16:1-23
		2	17:1a^{b}b, 4a^{b}b-7a, 10-12a^{b}b, 13b-16, 18ab^{b}, 20, 22a^{a}*, 24, 25a^{b}, 26a^{b}b, 28-30, 32a^{b}, 33-39, 42-48, 50-57a^{b}b
		3	18:1, 3-4, 5a^{a}b^{b}-19, 21-27a, 28-30
		4	19:1-24
		5	20:1-42
		6	21:1-16
		7	22:1-23
		8	23:1-28
		9	24:1-23
		10	25:1-44
		11	26:1-25
		12	27:1-12
		13	28:1-25
		14	29:1-11
		15	30:1-31
		16	31:1b, 4, 8-13
			II SAMUEL
		17	1:1-27
		18	2:1-32
	D	1	3:1-39
		2	4:1-12
		3	5:1b-3a, 4-25
		4	6:1-23
		5	7:1-4a, 5b-11, 13, 14b, 15b, 16b, 17a^{b}, 18-29
		6	8:1-18
		7	9:1-13
		8	10:1-19
		9	11:4-13, 20-21a, 25, 27a^{b}b
		10	12:1-24ab^{b}, 25-31
	E	1	13:2a^{b}, 3b, 12a^{b}b-13, 16-18, 19a^{b}, 20-22, 30b^{b}-31, 37-39
		2	14:1-33

Book	Part	Chap -ter	Fig 5 - The Dtr^2 History
			II SAMUEL
		3	15:4-7a, 8, 11, 12, 14-16, 17b, 18b-37
		4	16:1-23
		5	17:1-29
		6	18:2a, 5-8, 10b-14a, 16-18
		7	19:6b[b], 9b[b]-43
	F	1	20:1-26
		2	21:1-22
		3	22:1-51
		4	23:1-39
		5	24:1-25
VIII			I KINGS
	A	1	1:1-4, 6-8, 9a[b]b[b], 11-31, 35-37, 39a[a], 41b--48, 50-53
		2	2:1-9, 12-46a
		3	3:1-28
		4	4:1-20
		5	5:1-32
		6	6:1-38
		7	7:1-51
		8	8:1-66
		9	9:1-28
		10	10:1-29
		11	11:1-25, 27-39, 41
	B	1	12:2-3a, 5, 12, 15b-19, 20b-25, 27b, 28b, 30-33
		2	13:1-34
		3	14:1-20, 21b-24, 26a[b]b-29
		4	15:1, 3-7a, 9, 11-15, 21-23, 25-34
	C	1	16:1-34
		2	17:1-24
		3	18:1-46
		4	19:1-21
		5	20:1-43

Book	Part	Chap -ter	Fig 5 - The Dtr^2 History
			I KINGS
		6	21:1-29
		7	22:1-41, 43-44, 46-50, 52-54
			II KINGS
	D	1	1:1-18
		2	2:1-25
		3	3:1-27
		4	4:1-44
		5	5:1-27
		6	6:1-33
		7	7:1-20
	E	1	8:1-16, 18-23, 25, 27
		2	9:1-13, 14b-15, $16a^{b}b$, $21b^{b}$, $22b^{b}$, 25-26, 29-37
		3	10:1-36
		4	11:2b, $4b^{a}$, 5-11, $12a^{a}$, 14-15, $16a^{b}$, 17-20
		5	12:$2a^{a}$, 3-17, 20, $21b^{b}$, $22a^{a}$
		6	13:1-25
	F	1	14:1, 3-4, 6-18, 22-29
		2	15:1, 3-4, 6, 8-32, 34-37
		3	16:1, 2b-4, 6, 9b-19
		4	17:1-41
		5	18:1, 3-7a, 8, $9a^{b}$, $10a^{a}b^{a}$, 11b, $12a^{b}$, 14-16, $17b^{b}$, $27b^{b}$, 31-35, 36b-37
		6	19:1-7, 9b-35, $36a^{a}$
		7	20:1-21
	G	1	21:1-26
		2	22:1-20
		3	23:1-37
		4	24:1-20
		5	25:1-30

Part	Sect-ion	Fig 6 - The Ps Supplement
		LEVITICUS
I	A	1:1-3:17
	B	4:1-5:26
	C	6:1-7:38
II	A-D	[Lev 8:1 - 11:45 = Dtr^2]
		11:46-47
III	A	12:1-8
	B	13:1-59
	C	14:1-54
	D	15:1-33
	E	16:1-34
IV	A	17:1-18:30
	B	19:1-20:27
	C	21:1-22:33
	D	23:1-24:23
	E	25:1-26:46
	F	27:1-34

Fig 7 - The Composition of the Dtr History

J	P	E	Dtr^{2}
	GENESIS		
	1:1-31		
2:4b-7a, 8-9, 16-19a^{a}, 20b-22, 25	2:1-4a		2:7b, 10-15, 19a^{b}b-20a, 23-24
3:1-7a, 8-13, 22-23			3:7b, 14-20, 21, 24
			4:1-26
	5:1-29ab^{a}, 30-32		5:29b^{b}
6:1-2, 4a^{b}b, 4-6, 7a^{a}b, 8	6:9-22		6:3, 4a^{a}, 7a^{bg}
7:1a, 4, 7, 10, 16b, 17, 23a^{a}*b	7:6, 11, 13-16a, 18-21, 24		7:1b-3, 5, 8, 9, 12, 22, 23a*
8:6, 8-12	8:1-5, 13a, 14-19		8:7, 13b, 20-22
	9:1, 9-17, 28-29		9:2-8, 18-27
	10:1-7, 20, 22-23, 31-32		10:8-19, 21, 24-30
11:1-7, 8b, 9b	11:10-28, 31-32		11:8a, 9a, 29-30
12:1, 4a, 6a, 8a	12:4b-5		12:2-3, 6b, 7, 8b, 9-20
13:2, 5, 7a, 8-9a^{a}b, 10a, 11a, 12, 18a			13:1, 3-4, 6, 7b, 9a^{b}, 10b, 11b, 13, 14-17, 18b
			14:1-24
			15:1-21
	16:1, 3, 15-16		16:2, 4-14

Fig 7 - The Composition of the Dtr History

J	P	E	Dtr^{2}
		GENESIS	
	17:1-27		
18:1b, 2ab^{a}, 3-16			18:1a, 2b^{b}, 17-33
19:1a^{b}b^{a}, 2-8, 9a^{a}*b, 10, 12, 13a, 14, 24a, 25, 27a, 28			19:1a^{a}b^{b}, 9a*, 11, 13b, 15-23, 24b, 26, 27b, 29-38
		20:1a^{a}b, 2-3, 8, 10-11, 14-16	20:1a^{b}, 4-7, 9, 12-13, 17-18
21:1a, 2a, 3	21:1b, 2b, 4-5	21:6-10, 14-16, 19-20, 22-27a, 32, 34	21:27b-31, 33
		22:1-10, 13, 19	22:11-12, 14-18, 20-24
	23:1-20		
			24:1-67
	25:7-10, 12-17, 19-27, 29-30a, 31-34		25:1-6, 11, 18, 28, 30b
26:1a^{a}b, 6-9, 11-14, 16-17, 26-31			26:1a^{b}, 2-5, 10, 15, 18-25, 32-35
27:1-35, 36b-44, 45b			27:36a, 45a, 46
	28:1-5	28:10-12, 17-21a, 22	28:6-9, 13-16, 21b
29:1-13a, 15-23, 25-28, 30		29:13b-14	29:24, 29, 31-35
30:25-42		30:43	30:1-24

Fig 7 - The Composition of the Dtr History

J	P	E	Dtr^{2}
		GENESIS	
		31:1-2, 4-19a, 20-29, 36b, 38-47, 51-54	31:3, 19b, 30-36a, 37, 48-50
32:4-7, 14a, 25b, 27-29		32:1-3, 8-9, 14b-22, 23b, 24b	32:10-13, 23a, 24a, 25a, 26, 30-33
33:1a, 4, 12-16, 18a^{a}		33:3, 5, 8-11, 17	33:1b-2, 6-7, 18a^{b}b-20
			34:1-31
	35:9-13, 15, 27-29	35:1-7	35:8, 14, 16-26
	36:1-8a		36:8b-43
37:3a, 4, 12-13, 14ab^{b}, 15-18, 25-27, 28a^{b}	37:1, 2a^{a}*	37:2a^{b}b, 3b, 5-11, 19-24, 28a^{a}b, 29-36	37:2a^{g}, 14b^{a}
			38:1-30
39:1, 4a, 6a		39:4b, 6b, 7-20	39:2-3, 5, 21-23
		40:1-23	
41:54b		41:1-54a, 55-57	
42:1-4, 7-8, 9b-18a, 19-20, 24, 26, 29-34, 36, 38		42:5-6, 9a, 21-23	42:18b, 25, 27, 28, 35, 37
43:1-11, 13, 14b, 15a^{a}b, 16, 17, 23b, 24b-29a, 30-32a, 33			43:12, 14a, 15a^{b}, 18-23a, 24a, 29b, 32b, 34
			44:1-34

Fig 7 - The Composition of the Dtr History

J	P	E	Dtr^{2}
		GENESIS	
45:1-3, 24-25, 26a^{a}b, 27a^{a}b, 28		45:4-23	45:26a^{b}, 27a^{b}
46:28-34a	46:6-7	46:1-5	46:8-27, 34b
47:1-6	47:27-28	47:7-26	47:29-31
		48:1-2, 8-21	48:3-7, 22
	49:33b		49:1-33a
		50:1-8, 14-26	50:9-13
		EXODUS	
1:8-11a, 12a, 22	1:1-4, 5b, 7, 12b-14		1:5a, 6, 11b, 15-21
2:1-3, 5-6ab^{a}, 10a^{b}b^{a}, 11, 12, 15-21, 23a^{a}	2:23a^{b}b-25		2:4, 6b^{b}-10a^{a}b^{b}, 13-14, 22
3:2-4a, 7a, 8		3:1, 4b, 6a, 9-14	3:5, 6b, 7b, 15-22
4:19a^{b}b, 20a, 24-26		4:18	4:1-17, 19a^{a}, 20b-23, 27-31
			5:1-23
	6:2-12		6:1, 13-30
	7:1-13, 19-20, 21b-22		7:14-18, 21a, 23-29
	8:1-3, 9b-15		8:4-9a, 16-28
	9:8-12		
			10:1-29
	11:9-10		11:1-8

Fig 7 - The Composition of the Dtr History

J	P	E	Dtr^{2}
		EXODUS	
12:37a, 38	12:1-6, 8-11, 28, 40-42		12:7, 12-27, 29-36, 37b, 39, 43-51
13:20-22		13:17-19	13:1-16
14:5a, 6, 9a^{a}, 19b, 20, 24, 27b, 30	14:1-4, 8a, 9a^{b}b, 10b^{b}, 15-18, 21-23, 26, 27a, 28a, 29	14:5b, 7, 8b, 10ab^{a}, 19a, 25a, 28b	14:11-14, 25b, 31
	15:27		15:1-26
	16:1-3, 6-7, 9-15, 35a		16:4-5, 8, 16-34, 35b, 36
	17:1ab^{a}		17:1b^{b}-16
		18:1a, 2a, 3-5, 12-27	18:1b, 2b, 6-11
19:1b, 2b, 10a, 11 14b^{a}, 15a, 16a^{a}, 18ab^{a}, 20	19:1a, 2a	19:3a, 14a, 16a^{b}b-17, 18b^{b}-19	19:3b-9, 10b, 12-13, 14b^{b}, 15b, 21-25
		20:1	20:2-26
		21:2-37	21:1
		22:1-8, 20-30	22:9-19
		23:1-14, 15a^{a}*, 16, 20-22, 25b-31a	23:15a*b, 17-19, 23-25a, 31b-33
	24:15-18	24:13-14	24:1-12
	25:1-5, 8, 9a^{a}b		25:6-7, 9a^{b}, 10-40

Fig 7 - The Composition of the Dtr History

J	P	E	Dtr^2
		EXODUS	
	26:1-30		26:31-37
			27:1-21
			28:1-43
	29:43, 45-46		29:1-42, 44
			30:1-38
			31:1-18
		32:1-4, 6b, 15-21a, 22-25	32:5-6a, 7-14, 21b, 26-35
			33:1-23
34:5-7, 10-12a, 14, 19, 20b, 22, 24, 27		34:29b-32a, 33	34:1-4, 8-9, 12b, 13, 15-18, 20a, 21, 23, 25-26, 28, 29a, 32b, 34-35
	35:1a, 4b-7, 10, 20, 22-26, 29		35:1b-4a, 8-9, 11-19, 21, 27-28, 30-35
	36:2-38		36:1
			37:1-29
			38:1-31
			39:1-43
	40:16-19, 35b-37		40:1-15, 20-35a, 38

Fig 7 - The Composition of the Dtr History

J	P	Ps	Dtr^2
	LEVITICUS		
	1:1-17		
	2:1-16		
	3:1-17		
	4:1-35		
	5:1-26		
	6:1-23		
	7:1-38		
		8:1-36	
		9:1-24	
		10:1-20	
	11:46-47	11:1-45	
	12:1-8		
	13:1-59		
	14:1-54		
	15:1-33		
	16:1-34		
	17:1-16		
	18:1-30		
	19:1-37		

Fig 7 - The Composition of the Dtr History

J	P	Ps	Dtr^2
		LEVITICUS	
		20:1-27	
		21:1-24	
		22:1-33	
		23:1-44	
		24:1-23	
		25:1-55	
		26:1-46	
		27:1-34	
		NUMBERS	
			1:1-54
			2:1-33
			3:1-51
			4:1-49
			5:1-31
			6:1-27
			7:1-89
			8:1-26
			9:1-23
	10:11-12		10:1-10, 13-36

Fig 7 - The Composition of the Dtr History

J	P	Dtr[2]
	NUMBERS	
		11:1-35
	12:16b	12:1-16a
13:2a[a], 17-20, 22a, 23, 25a, 27-28, 30-31	13:1, 3, 21, 26a, 32, 33b	13:2a[b]b, 4-16, 22b, 24, 25b, 26b, 29, 33a
14:11a, 12-19a, 20, 21, 23-24	14:1a, 2-4, 26-32, 35-38	14:1b, 6-10, 11b, 19b, 22, 25, 33-34, 39-45
		15:1-41
16:12-14, 25a, 27b-32a, 33a, 34		16:1-11, 15-24, 25b-27a, 32b, 33b, 35
		17:1-28
		18:1-32
		19:1-22
20:14-18	20:1a[b], 2-5, 7-13, 22-25, 27, 28a[b]b, 29	20:1a[a]b, 6, 19-21, 26, 28a[a]
21:21-24		21:1-20, 25-35
22:2, 5-6, 36a, 40ab[a], 41	22:1	22:3-4, 7-35, 36b-39, 40b[b]
23:1-4, 5b, 6a, 7-9, 11-15, 16a[a]b, 17a[a]b, 18-20, 22, 24-30		23:5a, 6b, 10, 16a[b], 17a[b], 21, 23
24:1-3a, 5-6, 8a, 9, 10b, 11a, 25		24:3b-4, 7, 8b, 10a, 11b, 12-24

Fig 7 - The Composition of the Dtr History

J	P	Dtr^2
	NUMBERS	
		25:1-19
		26:1-65
	27:12-13, 15-21	27:1-11, 14
		28:1-31
		29:1-39
		30:1-17
		31:1-54
		32:1-42
		33:1-56
		34:1-29
		35:1-34
		36:1-13

Fig 7 - The Composition of the Dtr History

Dtr[1]	P	Dtr[2]
	DEUTERONOMY	
1:1a		1:1b-46
		2:1-37
		3:1-29
		4:1-49
5:1a[a]*, 2-4, 5*, 6-7, 9b-11, 24a, 25, 27		5:1*, 5, 8-9a, 12-23, 24b, 26, 28-33
6:4-9		6:1-3, 10-25
7:1-2ab[b], 17, 21, 23, 24		7:2b[ag], 3-16, 18-20, 22, 25-26
		8:1-20
		9:1-29
10:12, 14, 17, 18, 20		10:1-11, 13, 15-16, 19, 21-22
11:22-25a		11:1-21, 25b-32
12:13-14, 20, 26		12:1-12, 15-19, 21-25, 27-31
		13:1-19
14:4-5, 11-12, 13*, 16*, 17*, 18b-20, 22, 25-26		14:1-3, 6-10, 13*, 16*, 17*, 18a, 21, 23, 24, 27-29
15:19-20		15:1-18, 21-23
16:2a, 7a, 16a[a]b		16:1, 2b-6, 7b-15, 16a[b], 17-22
		17:1-20
		18:1-22

Fig 7 - The Composition of the Dtr History

Dtr^1	P	Dtr^2
	DEUTERONOMY	
		19:1-21
		20:1-20
		21:1-23
		22:1-29
		23:1-26
		24:1-22
		25:1-19
		26:1-19
		27:1-26
		28:1-69
29:1a, 9a, 11, 13-14		29:1b-8, 9b-10, 12, 15-28
		30:1-20
31:1, 2a, 3a, 6		31:2b, 3b-5, 7-30
	32:48-50, 52	32:1-47, 51
		33:1-29
	34:1a^{ag}b, 2-5, 7-9	34:1a^{b}, 6, 10-12

Fig 7 - The Composition of the Dtr History

Dtr^{1}	Dtr^{2}
JOSHUA	
1:1ab^{a}, 2-5ab^{b}	1:1b^{b}, 5b^{a}, 6-18
2:1-9a, 12ab^{a}, 13-16, 22-24a	2:9b-11, 12b^{b}, 17-21, 24b
3:5, 10b, 16b	3:1-4, 6-10a, 11-16a, 17
	4:1-24
	5:1-15
6:2, 16b, 20a^{a}b^{b}, 22, 23a^{a}, 25a^{a}b	6:1, 3-16a, 17-19, 20a^{b}b^{a}, 21, 23a^{b}, 24, 25a^{b}. 26-27
	7:1-26
8:1-2a^{a}b, 3ab^{a}, 4-5a, 6a^{a}b, 7, 9a^{a}, 11a, 16, 18, 18-19a*	8:2a^{b}, 3b^{b}, 5b, 6a^{b}b, 8, 9a^{b}b, 10, 11b-15, 17-18, 19a^{a}*, 19b-35
9:3-5, 8-9a^{a}, 12-13, 15a^{a}	9:1-2, 6-7, 9a^{b}-11, 14, 15a^{b}b-27
10:1a^{a}*b^{a}, 2-4a, 5, 8-9a, 10a	10:1a^{a}*, 4b, 6-7, 9b, 10b-43
11:1, 5, 6a, 8a^{a}*, 18, 23a^{a}b	11:2-4, 6b, 8*, 9-17, 19-22, 23a^{b}
	12:1-24
	13:1-33
	14:1-15
	15:1-63
	16:1-10
	17:1-18
	18:1-28

Fig 7 - The Composition of the Dtr History

Dtr^1		Dtr^2
	JOSHUA	
	19:1-51	
	20:1-9	
	21:1-45	
	22:1-34	
	23:1-16	
	24:1-33	
	JUDGES	
	1:1-36	
	2:1-23	
	3:1-31	
	4:1-24	
	5:1-31	
	6:1-40	
	7:1-25	
	8:1-35	
	9:1-57	
	10:1-18	
	11:1-40	
	12:1-15	

Fig 7 - The Composition of the Dtr History

Dtr^1	Dtr^2
JUDGES	
	13:1-25
	14:1-20
	15:1-20
	16:1-31
	17:1-13
	18:1-31
	19:1-30
	20:1-48
	21:1-25
I SAMUEL	
1:1-3a, 4-9a^a, 11ab^a, 11ab^a, 18b, 19a^{b}b, 20ab^a, 21, 22ab^a, 23a^{a}b, 24a^b	1:3b, 9a^{b}b, 10, 11b^b-18a, 19a^a, 20b^b, 22b^b. 23a^b, 24a^{a}b, 25-28
	2:1-36
	3:1-21
	4:1-22
	5:1-12
	6:1-21
	7:1-17

Fig 7 - The Composition of the Dtr History

Dtr^{1}	Dtr^{2}
I SAMUEL	
	8:1-22
9:1-$2a^{a}$, 3-$6a^{a}b$, 10, $14b^{a}$, 18, $19a^{a}$, 20a, 22a, 24b, 26b	9:$2a^{b}b$, $6a^{b}$, 7-9, 11-$14a^{a}$, $14b^{b}$-17, $19a^{b}b$, 20b-21, 22b-24a, 25-26a, 27
10:$10a^{a}$, 27b	10:1-9, $10a^{b}b$-27a
11:1-2a, $4a^{a}$, 9-10, 11a, 14a, $15a^{a}$	11:2b-3, $4a^{b}b$-8, 11b-13, 14b, $15a^{b}b$
	12:1-25
	13:1-23
14:52	14:1-51
	15:1-35
----------	----------
	16:1-23
17:$1a^{a}$, 2-$4a^{a}$, 7b-9, $12a^{a}$, 13a, 17, $18b^{a}$, 19, 21, $22a^{b}b$, 23*, $25a^{a}b$, $26a^{a}$, 27, 31, $32a^{a}b$, 40-41, 49, $57a^{a}$, 58	17:$1a^{b}b$, $4a^{b}b$-7a, 10-$12a^{b}b$, 13b-16, $18ab^{b}$, 20, $22a^{a}$, $23a^{a}$*, 24, $25a^{b}$, $26a^{b}b$, 28-30, $32a^{b}$, 33-39, 42-48, 50-$57a^{b}b$
18:2, $5a^{b}b^{a}$, 20, 27b	18:1, 3-4, $5a^{a}b^{b}$-19, 21-27a, 28-30
	19:1-24
	20:1-42
	21:1-16
	22:1-23
	23:1-28
	24:1-23
	25:1-44

Fig 7 - The Composition of the Dtr History

Dtr[1]	Dtr[2]
	I SAMUEL
	26:1-25
	27:1-12
	28:1-25
	29:1-11
	30:1-31
31:1a, 2-3, 4b-6	31:1b, 4, 7-13
	II SAMUEL
	1:1-27
	2:1-32
	3:1-39
	4:1-12
5:1a, 3b	5:1b-3a, 4-25
	6:1-23
7:4b-5a, 12, 14a, 15a, 16a, 17a[a]b	7:1-4a, 5b-11, 13, 14b, 15b, 16b, 17a[b], 18-29
	8:1-18
	9:1-13
	10:1-19
11:1-3, 14-19, 21b-24, 26-27a[a]	11:4-13, 20-21a, 25, 27a[b]b
12:24b[a]	12:1-24ab[b], 25-31

Fig 7 - The Composition of the Dtr History

Dtr^{1}	Dtr^{2}
II SAMUEL	
13:1-2a^{a}b, 3a, 4-12a^{a}, 14-15, 19a^{a}b, 23-29, 30ab^{a}, 32-36	13:2a^{b}, 3b, 12a^{b}b-13, 16-18, 19a^{b}, 20-22, 30b^{b}-31, 37-39
	14:1-33
15:1-3, 7b, 9-10, 13, 17a, 18a	15:4-7a, 8, 11-12, 14-16, 17b, 18b-37
	16:1-23
	17:1-29
18:1, 2b-4, 9, 10a, 14b-15, 19-32	18:2a, 5-8, 10b-14a, 16-18
19:1-6ab^{a}, 7-9ab^{a}	19:6b^{b}, 9b^{b}-43
	20:1-26
	21:1-22
	22:1-51
	23:1-39
	24:1-25
I KINGS	
1:5, 9a^{a}b^{a}, 10, 32-34, 38, 39a^{b}b, 40, 41a, 49	1:1-4, 6-8, 9a^{b}b^{b}, 11-31, 35-37, 39a^{a}, 41b-48, 50-53
2:10-11, 46b	2:1-9, 12-46a
	3:1-28
	4:1-20
	5:1-32
	6:1-38

Fig 7 - The Composition of the Dtr History

Dtr[1]	Dtr[2]
I KINGS	
	7:1-51
	8:1-66
	9:1-28
	10:1-29
11:26, 40, 42-43	11:1-25, 27-39, 41
12:1, 3b-4, 6-11, 13-15a, 20a, 26, 27a, 28a, 29	12:2-3a, 5, 12, 15b-19, 20b-25, 27b, 28b, 30-33
	13:1-34
14:21a, 25, 26a[a], 30-31	14:1-20, 21b-24, 26a[b]b-29
15:2, 7b-8, 10, 16-20, 24	15:1, 3-7a, 9, 11-15, 21-23, 25-34
	16:1-34
	17:1-24
	18:1-46
	19:1-21
	20:1-43
	21:1-29
22:42, 45, 51	22:1-41, 43-44, 46-50, 52-54
II KINGS	
	1:1-18
	2:1-25

Fig 7 - The Composition of the Dtr History

Dtr^{1}	Dtr^{2}
II KINGS	
	3:1-27
	4:1-44
	5:1-27
	6:1-33
	7:1-20
8:17, 24, 26, 28-29	8:1-16, 18-23, 25, 27
9:14a, 16a^{a}, 17-21ab^{a}, 22ab^{a}, 23-24, 27-28	9:1-13, 14b-15, 16a^{b}b, 21b^{b}, 22b^{b}, 25-26, 29-37
	10:1-36
11:1-2a, 3, 4ab^{b}, 12a^{b}b, 13, 16a^{a}b	11:2b, 4b^{a}, 5-11, 12a^{a}, 14-15, 16a^{b}, 17-20
12:1, 2a^{b}b, 18-19, 21ab^{a}, 22a^{b}t	12:2a^{a}, 3-17, 20, 21b^{b}, 22a^{a}
	13:1-25
14:2, 5, 19-21	14:1, 3-4, 6-18, 22-29
15:2, 5, 7, 33, 38	15:1, 3-4, 6, 8-32, 34-37
16:2a, 5, 7-9a, 20	16:1, 2b-4, 6, 9b-19
	17:1-41
18:2, 7b, 9a^{a}b, 10a^{b}b^{b}, 11a, 12a^{a}b, 13, 17ab^{a}, 18-27ab^{a}, 28-30, 36a	18:1, 3-7a, 8, 9a^{b}, 10a^{a}b^{a}, 11b, 12a^{b}, 14-16, 17b^{b}, 27b^{b}, 31-35, 36b-37
19:8-9a, 36a^{b}b, 37	19:1-7, 9b-36a^{a}
	20:1-21

Fig 7 - The Composition of the Dtr History

Dtr^1	Dtr^2
II KINGS	
	21:1-26
	22:1-20
	23:1-37
	24:1-20
	25:1-30

INDEX

A. Reference to Texts

GENESIS

DEUTERONOMY

B. Reference to Figures

DATE DUE